Customer Relationship Management

How to turn a good business into a great one!

Graham Roberts-Phelps

THOROGOOD

Reprinted by Thorogood 2003

10-12 Rivington Street, London EC2A 3DU

Telephone: 020 7749 4748

Fax: 020 7729 6110

Email: info@thorogood.ws

Web: www.thorogood.ws

A CIP catalogue record for this book is available
from the British Library.

ISBN 1 85418 119 X

Printed in India by Replika Press Pvt. Ltd.

About the author

Graham Roberts-Phelps is an experienced and professional business trainer and consultant, sharing his ideas and insights with thousands of people and organisations every year. With an extensive background in management and business development, he works with organisations of many different types and sizes.

Graham is the author of *Companies Don't Succeed – People Do!*, *Working Smarter* and *Telephone Tactics*, all published by Thorogood.

Contents

5

6

7

8

9

10

chapter one **Customer relationship management demystified**

What is customer relationship management?

You may have read other books and articles about customer relationship management, it is one of those phrases that are difficult to escape from hearing in business today – but what exactly is it? It seems to have a different meaning depending on whom you talk to. Is it a way of computerising your business? Is it a series of tools and techniques? Is it a marketing programme designed to attract customer loyalty? In its simplest form it is an attitude, a mindset, a value that you place on your business and its relationship with its customers. It is a methodology, a way of creating and evolving your organisation in the marketplace and at the same time in the mind of each individual customer. It must look at the whole process of what you're involved in, whether this is a product or a service driven organisation and it must involve every aspect of what you do – from suppliers through to the end application, from your internal staff through to your customer's customer. In its simplest form it recognises that each customer is an individual and has a choice. It looks at ways to treat customers more as individuals and to exercise their choice positively towards your organisation. It also embraces many current marketing and management methods, such as customer loyalty and marketing database management.

There are three main elements to consider when aligning your business towards a customer relationship format. The first is to do with retention. Imagine that you were never to gain another new customer, this would probably be a horrifying thought for most businesses, but when you considered it carefully you would realise that if you just kept the customers that you have then you would probably be able to grow and prosper in much the same way as you are now. There are of course exceptions. Most businesses only get a small percentage of the share of each of their customers. In addition most businesses will lose customers at a rate of somewhere between 15-50 per cent per annum. This leaky bucket effect is not only expensive, it is also reasonably unmotivating for the staff who have to serve these customers.

The second stage is to develop customer potential: turning that one off infrequent casual customer into a higher spending, more frequent, referring advocate.

The third element of customer relationship management and perhaps the most controversial one is the de-selection of customers. If a company or organisation were to put more of its efforts into its existing customers it would make sense that it did this with customers that had the greatest potential. This means that at some point, it has to start to lose those customers that are not ones that offer long-term future value. This might be because of transaction spend, the value of a customer or the cost of transacting or dealing with that customer or customer group.

In moving towards a more customer relationship orientated approach in your business there are some simple steps to help you along the way. However, before we look at these it is important to remember why customer lifetime value is so critical.

Customer lifetime value is typically the revenue that one customer can spend with you directly or through referral and recommendation over a nominal period of, say, ten years. A customer that buys once is probably doing so as a trial. The more frequently they come back to you the more their loyalty builds; they will then turn from a one-off customer into an ongoing client and eventually a self-perpetuating advocate. A loyal customer will often pay more as well; they will also be less sensitive to tactical discounting so that they will actually have more profitability than the customers that you attract through special offer promotions. Those customers that are attracted by special offer promotions will, of course, always be tempted by other special offer promotions and their loyalty can never be expected. The emotional link that a customer has with your organisation, the people that serve in it, or the brand that it promotes, are also critical factors in understanding customer loyalty and lifetime value.

The four steps to relationship management

The four steps to moving your organisation closer to a relationship based management programme are:

1. Segmentation
2. Analysing current behaviour
3. Developing strategy to achieve target behaviours
4. Behaviour maintenance.

By behaviour we mean the buying or other behaviours of a customer, in relationship to the organisation and its products and services.

In beginning the process it is probably worth taking time to do an audit of all the systems, information, research, marketing knowledge, attractiveness, historical results from promotions and any other additional sources of data that may exist in your organisation.

Customer relationship management requires a holistic approach so that the information that is held about customers across the organisation is drawn together in one central source or at least cross-accessed so that it can be compiled and collated. For example: information is probably held at an accounting level about customer transactions and appended to that may be a payment record. A different computer system may hold results of marketing activity for different customers or different customer groups. Another database may actually hold information on customer service queries or enquiries – times they may have phoned or contacted you for some question or other. This information needs to be carefully scoped and drawn together.

This analysis is the first part of segmentation by behaviour and value. The second stage is to begin an initial segmentation of a customer base. You should include the value, potential value and historical behaviour of your customer. This should then be compared with the existing buying patterns and behaviour and then contrasted, thirdly, with the future, or target behaviour, of an ideal or loyal customer.

Every customer is in some way unique. However, many customers are unique in similar ways. There are practical steps that can be taken to segment customers by value, pattern, and buying criteria.

EXAMPLE

A Chinese restaurant

A Chinese restaurant entrepreneur developed an informal but effective system for differentiating his customers. It intrigued him why some would return again and again, but others less frequently – and often the style and spend of their visits was inconsistent with previous visits. As a way of encouraging business he would try to remember details about his customers – children, what sort of car they drove, jobs, holidays etc. As his business expanded this became more difficult. Instead he transferred the information to card indexes and encouraged staff to do the same. He then began to add to this information the days of their visits, average spend, meal and wine preferences. As the system evolved he was also able to note preferences for tables and seating, dining times, and even preferred waiters and waitresses. Staff would often note down exact details, such as favourite flavourings and special requests.

How was this information used? Firstly, customers did not have to explain themselves as much as they would normally have done, and the level of personal service they received encouraged them to return to the restaurant even more frequently, and increased the average spend.

The restaurant owner also began to use the system in more sophisticated ways. He would design banquet evenings and ask selected customers to attend, almost as if they were invited guests. Because of the information he had gathered on each of them he was able to design and price the menus to match the expectations of each group. He would often charge the wealthier customers more for the same meal because he knew they would enjoy the evening better if they were paying more for it!

The next stage is to develop a strategy – a plan or a series of plans to attribute the target behaviour to each segment or individual – and then to begin to allocate a budget for each of those behaviours. For example, if you had a mail order business marketing collectible antique replicas, you would identify the different customer segments in terms of their buying behaviours and in terms of how much they had spent in the past; the frequency, the types of products that they had been interested in and the mechanisms that they had responded to – whether that's direct mail or off the page advertising, the Internet etc. If you were then trying to increase the frequency of spend or the transaction value of the spend, this would become a target behaviour that you would focus on.

The next stage is to look at the actual technology or systems that will allow you to achieve better relationship management with your customers. This may require some re-design or re-implementation of hardware and software to allow access to the information at a single point.

The final stage is a measurement in the evolution of the process. There is always a matter of trial and error and trial and success. Before implementing a wide scale programme it is essential that it is carefully tested on a small part of each segment of the customer base before being rolled out. Indeed by using customer relationship management methods in segmenting customers and customer groups more accurately, test marketing and test promotions can actually be far more accurately gauged and measured.

EXAMPLE

A successful hairdresser's salon

An example of a business employing a good relationship management strategy can be found in most high streets. In fact many businesses do it without even really thinking about it.

Some hairdressers are able to generate extraordinary levels of loyalty from their customers. This loyalty transcends such things as price differences and the convenience of their location. Many people will have their favourite hairdresser, someone they will return to again and again. Even when they have moved house or job, making that hairdresser less convenient, they may well still drive past dozens of other similar establishments to go there. Once they are there, only their favourite member of staff will do, even when the owner has trained that person. Once a salon has such loyalty from a customer it can charge increasingly more for its service.

Consider for a moment what this hairdresser might do to generate such loyalty – and profitability – from key customers. Their ability to cut, style and colour hair outstandingly is a given and usually not unique ability. The secret lies in their ability to manage every aspect of the relationship with the customer in such a way that the customer is always satisfied.

At the most obvious level the salon is always clean, stylish and attractive. Attention to detail ensures that first impressions become lasting impressions, from the coffee cups to the lack of coffee stains. The real differences between this and a less successful salon can be understood by looking at the business from the customer's perspective.

The customer's eye view

From the customer's viewpoint the organisation behaves like an ideal suitor. Their every need or wish is not only provided for but also anticipated and personalised. At every opportunity and interaction the customer is made to feel not only special, but also perhaps the most special and valued customer the organisation has.

In the hairdressing example, each and every customer experiences a slightly different version of the service and standards enjoyed by many. The stylists will know which of their customers like to talk and which topics they like to talk about. They will remember important things about each customer's life and lifestyle. Children, careers, holidays, favourite sports – each topic is carefully remembered and conversations continue from where they left off.

Treatments, products, styling and appointment times are seamlessly personalised for each customer. It is then a natural extension of this to target new products, services and special offers on particular customers. Customers selected in this way do not experience 'mass marketing' as we have come to know it.

Not only are offers personalised but so are letters, brochures and catalogues sent to them. Some customers may be contacted by phone, e-mail, mail or even in person, depending on their preference. The content, style and even the timing of such approaches can be tailored to fit a customer's unique 'buying fingerprint'. This is a set of parameters or attributes about how, when, where and what each customer buys.

In this environment the relationship the customer has with the organisation is well managed in a proactive way, making it exceptionally easy for the customer to do business and to remain a customer. It is also enjoyable for them – and profitable for the organisation.

In this way loyalty is not merely an absence of customer loss or erosion. Nor is it an attempt to generate short-term sales by marketing gimmicks. Instead it plays a natural part of a customer's behaviour and psychology. The drive and need for consistency is a strong emotional element in all our behaviours. Research has shown that customers who are treated in such a fashion will, over time, become blind to the marketing antics of competitors.

What this looks like in an organisation

These concepts appear simple and indeed it need not be any more complicated than this to understand, but changing your organisation to achieve it may not be quite so easy. While an owner-run establishment can track its most valued and profitable customers, this may not be so easy for a larger organisation.

Consider a car manufacturer trying to identify who its customers are, why they chose the make and model they did, then to manage their relationship through a third party dealership channel. Even trying to identify the end customer requires great resourcefulness. The car may have been purchased through a finance scheme or company car scheme, thereby creating real customer anonymity.

This example also begs the question of what it is the customer is loyal to. Is it the make of car – Mercedes, Mazda, or Ford – the model, the local dealership, or the relationship with the salesperson that sold it to them? In reality it might well be a complex interaction of all of them.

However, often the main challenge your organisation will face is not overcoming the physical hurdles of managing multiple and dispersed customer relationships. Decades of hit-and-run marketing practices and a culture that rewards sales rather than repeat customers will often be the biggest problem.

An organisation that takes customer relationship management seriously and operates it successfully is one where the customer becomes the central focus for all operations and decision-making.

The structure of your organisation or department must be customer-focused. For example, many companies will use a linear organisation chart to describe functions and job specifications. While this is a useful method of presenting information it does tend to reinforce a hierarchical approach. A better alternative is to visualise departments and job functions as interconnecting circles with the customer at the centre. In day-to-day practice this makes it much easier and much more satisfying for the customer to remain a customer.

Take the example of a simple garage repair workshop. The customers will have complete access to various functions – mechanic, supervisor, service receptionist, parts manager etc. They are not forced to deal with 'gatekeepers' or enforced procedures. Similarly the vehicle technician or stores assistant can deal with the customer directly and indeed is required to do so should the need arise. So if the car is not going to be ready at the specified time, the first person to recognise this phones the customer and explains why. On collecting the vehicle the customer can discuss any aspect of the work directly with the technician or mechanic who worked on it. There is no reason why this should not be replicated throughout the dealer network or organisation and be continued through to include the car manufacturer.

Not just another marketing trick

Many companies are now discovering that customer relationship management is not something that you can simply bolt onto a business. In a democratised market it is the quality and depth of the customers' relationships – physically and psychologically – that ultimately differentiates between brands.

Advances in technology, plus the price advantages gained through global location, better purchasing and sophisticated marketing methods, make it harder to differentiate yourself from your competitors now than at almost any time in living memory.

Traditional marketing wisdom over the last 20 years has had it that buyers are likely to react in a Pavlovian manner to price cuts, special offers and other inducements. It is a common moan, especially in the retail sector, that customers respond only to price – then shop around for even sharper bargains.

An interesting example is the way Internet businesses were able to attract customers easily and quickly in the late nineties for products such as books and CDs. The traditional providers and marketers of these goods had failed to build any lasting or real relationships with their customers. Most of them did not know who their customers were, and even if they wanted to have a dialogue with them they would not have had enough information to do so.

The very term 'customer loyalty' is a flawed one. Customer loyalty programmes often have the opposite effect to that intended. Research has shown that if a customer carries one store card they will probably carry three or four others. There are exceptions, of course, but in many cases these schemes simply confuse the customer and waste profits.

There are other reasons why customer loyalty marketing is not as effective as it was hoped it would be:

► There are just too many programmes – everyone offers them!

► Programmes are frequently focused on short-term rewards not longer term benefits

► Few programmes seem to really understand the needs, views and ideas of their customers

► There is often little intelligent segmentation – everybody is assigned to the same loyalty programme, when in reality there are different reasons why some customers remain with the organisation and others do not

► There is no, or only a limited, opportunity for dialogue and interaction with customers

► The loyalty programmes are seldom allowed to evolve and instead are simply replaced with something 'new and improved'

► Customers are increasingly cynical about such programmes

► Companies lack the emotional or financial commitment to make the programmes work.

A customer loyalty programme, just like a quality programme, is only one tool or method in managing a customer's relationship and delivering customer satisfaction. There is far more to gain from fostering good principles than from investing in such expensive and complicated schemes.

The business case

As has been mentioned, the customer's relationship with an organisation or brand is as important, if not more important, than product or price advantages. Research suggests that it costs five times more to attract a new customer than it does to keep an old one. Consider for a moment the cost of marketing, sales, commissions, accountancy, administration, credit and bad debt collection for a new customer, and contrast this with the non-recurring costs for repeat customers.

This is only the tip of the iceberg. If you factor in the amount of additional business one satisfied customer can bring you, the case for building a customer relationship management strategy becomes compelling. Consider the following example:

The weekly supermarket trip

Most families visit a local supermarket regularly for groceries. This choice is often made either by habit or by unconscious selection – perhaps a preference for the location or store layout, or loyalty to a brand, organisation or card points scheme.

With some effort it should be possible to calculate the approximate cost of attracting new customers to any particular location. The repeat visit by a customer need not cost anything, as the overheads have been accounted for in previous marketing. If a typical family were to spend, say, £100 a week on average on groceries, the supermarket should then begin to measure their share of that customer's business – which is more important than what share of the local marketplace they perhaps attract. This £100 a week spend is £5,200 per year and £52,000 over ten years. Add to this how many other customers they might influence to shop there, such as family members, friends and neighbours, this word-of-mouth factor is an important consideration.

As the organisation, in this case the supermarket, begins to learn more about the customer because of the closer relationship it is able to forge, it can better stock, equip, staff and manage the store to serve more than the customer's needs. Special offers, discount vouchers and even opening times can be altered to suit different segments and types of customers. For example, a family might spend a significant amount on dog and cat food and therefore receive vouchers for these items. The supermarket is also able to analyse the gaps in the customer's shopping trolley. These are products they might well be buying elsewhere.

In this way the supermarket does not discount products unnecessarily – items that the customer was going to buy from it anyway – but instead targets offers strategically, to grow the customer's spending. The role of customer relationship management is not simply an additional marketing device or tool, but a complete philosophy that must replace the hunter-gatherer mentality of many modern marketing methods.

Another example of where customer relationship management can increase profitability is in its ability to segment customers. This means you would decide which customers you would like to foster relationships with, and conversely those with whom you do not want to build long-term relationships with. This could be for a variety of reasons. In many cases it might simply not be worth it – although customer relationship management does better equip your organisation to develop small or one-off customers into more loyal, high-spending advocates of your business. Another reason could be that some customers might divert attention and resources away from the core business. Recent moves by a retail financial organisation in this area have led to new charges and systems for some customers and savings and improvements for others. This trend is sure to continue.

chapter two Why do customers defect?

Introduction

Consider for a moment what you would have to do to lose all your customers. The list might include some or all of the following:

- ▶ Ignore them
- ▶ Lie to them
- ▶ Fail to return calls or answer letters or e-mails
- ▶ Fail to deliver on promises
- ▶ Miss expectations
- ▶ Be rude to them
- ▶ Stop all marketing activity
- ▶ Patronise them
- ▶ Fail to open on time or be available at the right times
- ▶ Not listening to them
- ▶ Poor follow-up
- ▶ Incompetent staff
- ▶ Poor product quality
- ▶ Confusing pricing
- ▶ Treating them as if they were in the wrong.

You can probably think of others – perhaps something one of your customer service or sales staff would do while working out their notice period!

The stark reality is that many organisations lose a significant proportion of their customer base every single year and either don't know who these customers are, why they are leaving or spending less, or don't care!

Why are customers lost?

Many surveys have been carried out over recent years to try to understand why customers defect. While the answers may vary by customer and organisation, survey after survey highlights similar trends and reasons.

Price

While it may be important in attracting new customers, it would seem that it is a minor issue in developing loyalty and retaining customers. Most research in this area, though varying by industry and country, rarely puts price at more than 15 per cent as the reason for switching suppliers or business.

Physical factors

Such physical factors as a 'more convenient location' are also ranked quite low, as are competitor action and invention. Marketing and competitor activity and a relationship with a competitor are about 15 per cent. The competitor product's advantages can often account for the further 10 to 15 per cent.

However, one of the most common and significant reasons for customer switching and disloyalty is the **indifference and inattention of the business** and, from the customer's point of view, the lack of any real reason to stay. Most surveys highlight poor service as a more common reason for switching suppliers than price advantage.

This can also be supported by the general observations of marketing specialists, who detect the following changes in consumer and business purchasing behaviour:

Customer sophistication

Customers not only expect and demand more they are also more articulate in saying so. Twenty years of dramatic social change – in housing, lifestyle, education, travel etc – have changed the way many of us select the businesses we use.

Complexity

Buying even the simplest product or service can, if the customer wishes, be a very complex decision-making process. The blurring of differences between brands, products and companies; the dynamic interaction between a product and the level of service behind it, both during a sale and afterwards, make it difficult to isolate buying motivations and criteria.

Competition

In almost every market in every developed country of the world, competition has increased dramatically in the last ten years. Globalisation, advanced manufacturing technology and many other factors have led to business becoming faster, having a higher quality, being quicker to innovate and being more price-competitive etc.

Consider the personal computer industry

From two or three main hardware manufacturers in the early eighties, there are now thousands of organisations producing an almost infinite variety of options and possibilities. Players move into the market and can quickly gain advantage and market share, at least for a brief period.

Costs

Cost has a significant role to play in understanding the economic trends and changes of recent years. The economic downturn of the early nineties gave both the business customer and personal consumer a sharp jab in the ribs to remind them that markets can indeed go down as well as up. This experience and the lingering memory of it have made us all more aware of cost; the value of managing cost, and the importance of getting greater value for money when purchasing and choosing suppliers.

If we look in more detail at what is meant by 'indifference', both through the research statistics and our own experience, it becomes clear that there are many critical aspects behind any customer defection, including:

▶ Too little contact

▶ Too little individual attention

▶ Poor quality attention – especially when problems are encountered

▶ Generally poor service levels and standards.

In non-commercial organisations or utility providers, where changing supplier or switching business is more difficult, these four factors are often at the root of the majority of complaints.

The obvious, common sense deduction is that improving these four areas will encourage customers to stay. But this is not the case. Improvement in these four areas usually reduces the amount of customer erosion or 'churn', but further steps are usually needed to create loyal, higher-spending customers.

EXAMPLE

Mercedes Benz

Mercedes Benz enjoys a reputation as one of the world's leading car makers. It also boasts a high level of customer loyalty and advocacy. As an example, over a third of all new car customers choose to take advantage of the company's offer to collect the car in person from the factory. An extensive customer centre delivers a high level of hospitality, allowing them a factory tour and presentations about the organisation's history and development. Customers even have an opportunity to talk with the technicians who carry out the final preparation of their vehicle. Many of these customers travel from all over the world for this experience.

Complacency, not competition, kills customers

As many successful organisations are now discovering to their cost, the challenge to their future is not necessarily from their competitors, but from their own complacency towards their customers. These organisations become victims of their own success. Although this is not typically a new phenomenon, it is an increasing one. As an example, in America, General Electric was the market leader in valve-based products during the 1960s and 1970s, and therefore rejected diversifying into new transistor and chip-based developments.

Another more recent example was the fall from grace during the late nineties of the unique and successful Marks and Spencer organisation. Typically regarded as one of the best run retailing organisations in the world, it has suffered at the hands of its customers. Marks and Spencer was probably the last to realise what many customers knew already – it had become complacent. Once the scale of the problem had been realised the chief executive admitted openly to a meeting of City brokers that they had indeed 'lost the plot' in their relationship with their customers. The St Michael brand no longer meant the same thing to a new generation of discerning customers, and existing customers were far more flirtatious than they had been.

Perhaps one of the reasons for this happening was that market research and customer surveys had focused on only a small number of relatively loyal customers. This meant that the company did not get early warning of trouble.

Among the measures Marks and Spencer is taking to put things right, are a better relationship with its customers, including more accurate segmentation; more frequent interaction and attention to innovation and service standards.

However, Marks and Spencer is not unique, and there are many similar experiences by companies of all sizes in all markets. One of the biggest blocks in building solid customer relationships is an organisation taking its finger off the pulse of what customers want. The other side of this coin is the belief that an organisation knows what its customers want. It is interesting that so many marketing, service and product innovations are by insurgent, expanding and hungry upstarts in a market, rather than the incumbent market leaders.

No organisation should think of itself as immune. You can be IBM, BMW, Coca-Cola, Levi's, Disney, Virgin Group or even Microsoft, but complacency is what gives opportunity to competitors.

The service economy

The reality of today's service-based and customer-focused economic world is in marked contrast to the attitudes and priorities that previously existed in organisations. Following here is a review of the main elements that organisations should be grasping in order to deliver solid customer relationships:

Priority of service

Necessary evil – or top management concern?

In traditional, product-based and marketing-led organisations this was always seen as a rather incidental or necessary evil. Today it must become a top management concern. In transforming British Airways from an engineering-based, product-led organisation to a successful global airline differentiating on customer service, Colin Marshall, then chief executive, made customer service issues a regular boardroom discussion. He would insist on travelling as the mystery customer in the early days of the transformation, and would often arrive unannounced at airport check-in desks. He would also spend periods working with staff to understand the service issues.

Method of service

Corrective action – or customer-driven service management?

The second significant difference between a customer-centric and a product-led organisation is the method of service. Is your company's based on company policy, preferences and procedures – or customer-driven measures and standards? Does your organisation do the minimum required to solve a customer's problem, or look to solve the problem and maintain goodwill and a positive relationship?

Customer requirements

Unknown or assumed – or researched regularly and the basis for decisions?

Detailed knowledge and understanding of customer requirements – physical and psychological – are required to manage customer relations well. To begin with these requirements may be unknown or guessed at. There may also be an assumption that the requirements and needs of yesterday's customers will also apply to today's and tomorrow's. As we have seen, this is a dangerous attitude. Instead, customers' requirements should be sought, analysed and acted upon and business decisions must be based on such information. It is also important that the varying requirements of different customers, both individually or by segment, are fully understood and delivered.

Strategies and systems

Serve organisational needs – or serve customer needs?

One of the most vocal and outspoken critics of quality programmes and Total Quality Management (TQM) procedures is Tom Peters. While acknowledging the need for high quality and 'doing things right' he says this is no guarantee of customer satisfaction, financial success or loyalty. A good example of this is a large telecommunications company that boasted in its annual report of a significant improvement in the speed of handling customer complaints and problems. This included the implementation of call handling and computer systems. The name of the department was changed from 'complaints' to 'customer service'. The futility of this achievement only really became apparent when a journalist suggested that it might have been better to spend the time and energy preventing problems and complaints rather than solving them.

chapter three The economics of customer care

Introduction

The provision of excellent customer care is important as it allows you to build a strong, loyal relationship with your customers. The information in this chapter will help you to understand how to form this relationship, so the loyalty of a customer will be ensured for many years.

Know what your customers are worth

Firstly, let us look at how you can calculate the true value of your existing customers. Many businesses spend about 75 per cent of their marketing budget in a search for more new customers. The cost of this marketing mistake is a negative effect on profits. It is a mistake because:

► It costs substantially more to win a new customer than it does to keep a current customer

► The longer a business keeps a customer, the more profitable that customer is for the business

► As a customer's lifetime value grows, the more dependent they become on a company, and the less susceptible they are to other companies' offers of lower prices

► As customers become more loyal, they can become advocates for the business, encouraging friends and acquaintances to also buy there.

You need to understand the lifetime value of your customers, and communicate this throughout the enterprise.

Customer value calculation

The following value formula worksheet will help you to calculate the average lifetime value of each customer in your facility:

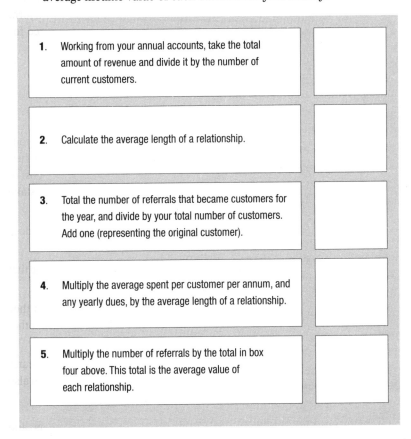

1. Working from your annual accounts, take the total amount of revenue and divide it by the number of current customers.

2. Calculate the average length of a relationship.

3. Total the number of referrals that became customers for the year, and divide by your total number of customers. Add one (representing the original customer).

4. Multiply the average spent per customer per annum, and any yearly dues, by the average length of a relationship.

5. Multiply the number of referrals by the total in box four above. This total is the average value of each relationship.

Figure 1: A value formula worksheet

While this calculation does over simplify the issue, it is useful in high-lighting the value of a customer. Especially when you consider that customer attrition (loss) can be anywhere from 15 to 50 per cent.

The cost of replacing one customer is the sum of all marketing and sales costs for the year, divided by the number of new customers attracted. For example, marketing and sales costs: £55,000 (includes all salaries, fixed overheads, variable costs, etc) producing 200 new customers, replacement cost: £275. Therefore if each customer pays on average monthly dues of £50, it will be nearly six months before the marketing costs have been covered. If you add the costs of providing facilities and staff, this is even longer.

Profit per customer is achieved when marketing costs have been paid. Every month or year that a customer stays a customer, they become more valuable.

Total impact on your bottom line

If you take the average value and divide by twelve, you will know how much revenue each customer is worth for each extra month that they remain a customer. If you take the average monthly value and multiply it by the number of customers you have, you will know how much impact keeping every customer for one month longer will have on your bottom line.

As an exercise, use the following data in the previous worksheet to calculate the customer value:

1. Annual revenue from customer subscriptions: **£1.2 million**

2. Number of customers: **2,000**

3. Additional revenue from shop sales and other items: **£75,000**

4. Average length of customer relationship: **3 years**

5. Number of referral customers for the past year: **250**

Building a loyal relationship

If you can build a truly customer-orientated business that treats customers as individuals and focuses on their lifetime value, you can move from purchase transactions to transformational relationships – in other words, numerous ways to increase profitability while decreasing the cost of doing business.

While the stress will always be on delivering a personalised service to your customers, there are some general things you should do – and some you should avoid:

Examples of bad service

▶ Allowing the telephone to ring for an extended period of time, i.e. more than three rings.

▶ Unhelpful comments such as 'It's not my job'.

▶ The enterprise is unclean, floors not swept in changing rooms etc.

▶ Not notifying customers of changes concerning their status.

▶ Not delivering what has been promised.

Examples of good service

▶ Responding to customers' needs quickly and efficiently.

▶ Implementing loyalty programmes.

▶ Having a suggestion box on the reception desk.

▶ Having staff who are polite, helpful and friendly at all times.

▶ Following the philosophy that 'nothing is too much trouble'.

Tips to ensure success

There are some important steps that you should take to ensure that your enterprise provides better customer service.

Know what each customer expects from the enterprise:

- **Customer product** – high quality every time, preferably above expectations

- **High perceived value** – attention to detail and added service touches

- **Clear benefits** – stated and personalised

- **Reliability** – no broken equipment, or promises

- **Customer service** – responsive and knowledgeable

- **Guarantee/warranty** – deliver what you promise 'or your money back'

- **Accessibility** – everybody should be available to talk to a customer

- **Complaint resolution** – fast response always

- **Positive experiences** – don't serve your customers, delight them.

It might be useful to think of each customer as having certain 'life cycle stages'.

1. Contact phase

Goal: to gain a new customer. Contact through marketing, advertising, telemarketing, personal selling, direct mail, promotions, and publicity.

2. Acquisition phase

Goal: to increase customer retention. Collect as much information about the customer as possible. Understand their purchase condition. Offer them post-purchase reassurance. Promote the price-value relationship. Establish the foundation for a long-term relationship. Know the associated costs.

3. Retention phase

Goal: to create long-term, committed and loyal customers. Develop a service philosophy. Increase the responsiveness to customers. Identify and close service gaps. Improve the service recovery process. Measure customer satisfaction. Reward positive customer behaviour. Know your retention-related costs.

4. Loyalty phase

Goal: to extend your customer's loyalty. Define loyalty and customer lifetime. Know their lifetime value and average net worth. Counteract defection rates and patterns. Understand loyalty calculations. Know your costs associated with their loyalty. Provide them with accurate customer information. Ensure that you know your products inside out and back to front! Communicate with the customer. Learn about the customer. Provide value on every contact. Reward the customer's loyalty.

Twelve ways to stay close to your customers

1. **Show them that you think of them**. Send or fax helpful newspaper clippings, relevant articles, and Christmas and birthday cards. How about sending a card on the anniversary of the day they became your customers?

2. **Tell them what's new**. It is a good way to stay in touch and increase sales or get referrals.

3. **Offer 'valued customer' discounts**. These can take the form of coupons, letters, or other sales promotions. This not only garners more orders; it also makes your customers happy to be getting such good deals.

4. **Compensate customers** for lost time or money if they were caused by problems with your product or service. Use a well thought-out recovery programme and stick to it. Better to err on the side of generosity than lose an account out of stinginess!

5. **Be personal**. Keep notes in your customer files on every little detail you know – everything from spouse and children's names to hobbies, and especially their behavioural style.

6. **Always be honest**. Nothing undermines your credibility more severely than dishonesty. Lies have a way of coming back to haunt you.

7. **Accept returns unconditionally**. The few pounds you might lose in the short run are far less than what you gain from pleasing the customer.

8. **Honour your customer's privacy**. If you have been a truly consultative salesperson, you may possess some knowledge that should be kept confidential. Your ethical standards should demand that you keep it that way.

9. **Keep your promises**. Never, ever promise something that you cannot deliver. This principle applies to little things such as returning phone calls as well as big things like delivery dates. If you must, 'baby-sit' deliveries and promised service to see that they are realised. Your reputation is on the line.

10. **Give feedback on referrals**. This is the right way to show your appreciation for the referral. Tell your customer the outcome. This is also a good way to get more referrals without asking for them directly.

11. **Make your customers famous ...for 15 minutes**. If your enterprise has a newsletter, ask customers for permission to write about their successes. Then send a copy to your customer. The same can be done for local newspapers and other publications.

12. **Keep lines of communication open**. As in any relationship, assure your customers that you are open to all calls about everything and anything – ideas, grievances, advice, praise, questions etc. This is one way to maintain that all-important rapport.

Remember that people do business with people they like!

Exercise: Customer dynamics

How does your enterprise rate? Try to complete this questionnaire to rate your company and the service it provides to its customers.

1. **Responsiveness**. Do customers get 'sheep-dip' service or does your company treat people as individuals?

   Low
   1 2 3 4 5
   6 7 8 9 10
   High

2. **Competence.** Does your company have an image of expertise in which customers can place their trust?

   Low
   1 2 3 4 5
   6 7 8 9 10
   High

3. **Reliability.** How dependable is your product or service? How well does your company follow through on promises?

   Low
   1 2 3 4 5
   6 7 8 9 10
   High

4. **Relationship.** How well does your company show customers that it cares and wants long-term relationships with them?

   Low
   1 2 3 4 5
   6 7 8 9 10
   High

5. **Accuracy.** How well does your company avoid mistakes, especially expensive or time-consuming mistakes?

   Low
   1 2 3 4 5
   6 7 8 9 10
   High

6. **Personal service.** How well do service representatives and other front-line people show customers that they are special?

   Low
   1 2 3 4 5
   6 7 8 9 10
   High

7. **Courtesy.** Does everyone in your company treat customers with this most basic ingredient of human interaction and service?

   Low
   1 2 3 4 5
   6 7 8 9 10
   High

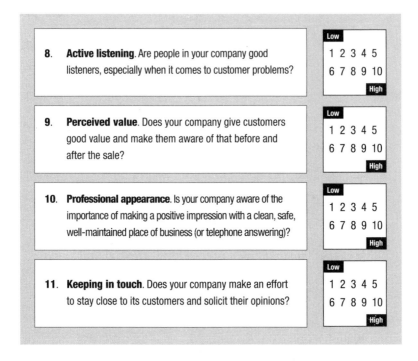

Figure 2: Customer dynamics questionnaire

Customer attrition and retention

Attrition is the key indicator in measuring the success of any retention and customer service strategy. It is a monthly performance indicator that should be acted upon sooner rather than later.

Relationship attrition is the number of customers who do not renew their relationship in any one-month, expressed as a percentage of the number of customers at the start of the month.

Each organisation will have its own means of measurement that relates to its management systems, but as long as this is consistent, it is only the fluctuations that are relevant.

The measure of relationship retention is an important indicator of how effective your organisation is in meeting the desires of your customers. In some instances, the rate at which people stop attending on a regular basis or fail to renew their relationship can be very high.

Take the example of a fitness centre. During its early years, renewal rates were as low as 20 per cent with a corresponding attrition rate of 80 per cent. Such a low renewal rate carried an important message: a lot of people had a desire to become involved in health and fitness. They also thought a particular enterprise would provide an answer to their need and were sold on it. Unfortunately, the experience was not meeting their expectations so they did not renew their relationship.

Working out your attrition and retention rates

How do you know that the efforts you are making are actually achieving the results you want in terms of keeping customers?

Over the last few years, many formulas have been devised to look at the data available from computer systems. No matter which you use, the most important factor is consistency from year to year. This is the only way to ensure that you are comparing apples with apples and can measure significant fluctuations in your market.

EXAMPLES

The International Health, Racquet and Sports Enterprise Association (IHRSA) uses the following formula to track retention:

Attrition (per cent) = [Number of customers lost during a given period (year/month)] ÷ [number of customers at start of same period] x 100.

Another enterprise uses an even simpler formula:

[Number of cancellations x 12] ÷ [number of customers at the beginning of the month].

A number of considerations may affect your totals. For example, do you count customer 'holidays' or 'freezes'? What about summer customers? What happens when you have a spurt of business due to outside factors (e.g. another enterprise in your town goes out of business and you absorb their customers) or a loss of business due to uncontrollable factors (your pool springs a leak and you have to subsidise your customers' use of another facility until you can repair yours)? How do you track uncontrollable as opposed to potentially controllable factors (people who leave due to a move or loss of job versus those who resign because they are unhappy with the service you are providing)?

Attrition formulas will give you a base of information to look at from one period to the next, but may not always provide an accurate picture of what is going on with your customers. What you really want to know is whether the customer who started last year will remain with you one, two or three years later.

As we have seen, your aim is to keep customers for as long as possible. So, if a customer were to stay with you for 15 months, the goal would be to keep them for 16 months, then 17 months and so on. For each additional month you retain that customer, you increase your profit margin, all other factors being equal. The critical months are the first four-month period and then the five to eight-month period. This can be thought of as moving a customer from 'infant' to 'independent'. To increase retention, focus on moving new customers from the 'infant' stage to the 'independent' stage. One of the best ways to implement this is to allocate sales, customer service or other staff as 'customer assistants'. Each would be assigned 150 to 200 customers each. It is then their job to work with the customers, keep in touch and direct them to products or services until they are familiar enough with what you are offering to be 'independent'. Computer technology can help significantly in tracking customers through this life cycle.

For example, some fitness centres now use computer systems that enable customers to check in at a kiosk and enter information about their activities and lifestyle for the day (or week, etc). The customer can then get a personalised lifestyle prescription for the next week that will keep them on a path to achieve their goals. Impressively, the combination of such a computer facility and the customer assistants programmes has been shown to yield a reduction in the drop out rate during the first eight months from 50 per cent to 20 per cent.

Based on such an approach, an alternative to the standard retention formulas is to look at the average length of a relationship and to try to extend it. Using whatever computer records you have (if you keep expired records on your computer), examine the contracts of your former customers and determine the length of time they were with you. Calculate the average by totalling all of the durations, and divide by the number of former customers. This can be quite a task, so look only at the last five years (at most).

Once this has been done, you will have a base average to work with and you can start identifying existing customers that might be at risk of leaving. Pull reports for customers who have not been active in the last 30, 60 or 90 days, and phone them up. But be careful how you do this. If you call and say, 'Hey, you haven't been in lately...' You might run the risk of their saying, ' You're right! I've been meaning to cancel this relationship!' Whoops!

A more advisable, softer approach would be to call the 'at-risk' customers and invite them to come in for a specific reason. Best of all, of course, is that if you have compiled a profile of them, you can start with a topic you know interests them. If you don't have a profile on them, you can tell them you're calling customers at random to tell them about new products and to get their feedback.

These calls can then serve the multiple purposes of getting people signed up for events, notifying them about programmes, products or services and, not least, to gain feedback about any changes you could make to keep them more involved. The contact alone is often enough to keep a relationship going for one to two months longer than you might have otherwise.

Exit questionnaires

Where appropriate to your business, exit questionnaires can provide a great deal of useful information. Try to categorise reason and allocate codes to them. They should fall into two main groupings:

1. Uncontrollable

House move, death, illness, loss of income, non-payment of relationship fees (uncollectable).

2. Controllable

Not using, no time, too expensive.

If your enterprise's controllable attrition rate reaches more than 15 per cent of the total exit questionnaires in any given period, you can start to worry. For example, if you lost 20 customers in one month, and more than seven were due to controllable factors, you would have to revisit your retention programme.

Customer service surveys

Customers have invested their time and sought services from you because they believe that you can satisfy their desires. Their opinions concerning how they feel and how your services could be improved or developed are valuable.

Someone might continue to visit your business because they have paid a relationship fee and wish to receive the benefit they have purchased. But they might not be completely satisfied with the services provided and have no desire to renew the relationship. By asking for their opinions, you might be able to understand how to satisfy their desires more completely and so retain customers that would otherwise not return.

Valuable feedback can be obtained through questionnaires or interviews, and staff should be in a position to pass on comments that have been made about your services.

A questionnaire sent out in the post or by e-mail cannot be as comprehensive as that used for a personal interview. Since there will be no interviewer at hand to explain the questions they must be put in an elementary manner and require as little writing as possible on the part of the respondent. The normal method is either to frame questions which require a simple 'yes' or 'no' answer, or to provide several alternative answers to each question, asking respondents to mark the one they consider most applicable.

One of the main difficulties with the use of postal questionnaires is that only about one person in ten will take the trouble to respond. Furthermore, the fact that they have taken this trouble, whereas nine out of ten have not, suggests that they are probably not typical.

You can use various devices to encourage people to respond – such as a free gift attached to the survey or a free prize draw for those who return the questionnaires.

Like all unsolicited direct mail approaches – of which this is just a specialised category – the accompanying letter of explanation must be written in such a way that the customer is urged to make the effort to complete the questionnaire and post it back. The letter must explain the purpose of the survey in terms that the customer can understand and, ideally, which will excite some interest on their part.

How to keep a customer for life

- ▶ Select the right customers through market research.
- ▶ Know your purpose for being in business.
- ▶ Move customers from satisfaction to loyalty by focusing on retention and loyalty schemes.
- ▶ Develop reward programmes.
- ▶ Customise your products and services.
- ▶ Train and empower your employees in excellent customer service.

- ▶ Respond to customers' needs with speed and efficiency.
- ▶ Measure what's important to the customer – always add value.
- ▶ Know exactly what customers want in their relationship with you.
- ▶ Know why customers leave your enterprise by producing customer exit surveys.
- ▶ Conduct a failure analysis on your enterprise.
- ▶ Know your retention improvement measures – have a strategy in place.
- ▶ Use market value pricing concepts.
- ▶ Do what works all over again!

Remember!

96 per cent of unhappy customers never complain.

But if their problem remains unsolved – they usually tell ten other customers!

chapter four Defining customer service excellence

Nothing impresses like competence

Before you start using any particular tricks, techniques, promotions or special devices to keep your customers, 'your customers', there is one inescapable fact: nothing impresses a customer like competence.

Customers go back to businesses that they like. They go back to businesses that they enjoy dealing with, they enjoy people who are nice to them and they enjoy people who work hard to keep them satisfied. This is not a particularly difficult idea; in fact it should seem just like common sense. However, the paradox is that common sense is not common practice. A short discussion with a group of people about customer service, no matter who they are, will soon detect and define a huge number of unsatisfied customer needs, requirements and experiences. Contrast that with those experiences or situations where we've received, what might be called, exceptional customer service, for example, times when we've had an experience which was outstanding and that some way went over and above what we'd previously expected, and those experiences will almost certainly be fewer in number.

There is also a psychological principle here, in that we often remember bad things more than good things. It may also be because so much of customer service falls into the category of indifference.

Survey after survey has highlighted that there are only three major types of customer experience. The first is 'hospitable' or 'friendly' or 'exceptional' customer service, which may account for 10-15 per cent in a reasonable sample. At the other end of the scale is a service experience that might be termed as 'rude' or 'unsatisfactory', once again, this may be between 10 and 15 per cent. The vast majority of our experiences as customers and the vast majority of the experience of your customers, no matter what business you're in, will almost certainly be that of indifference. The challenge that I often hear from managers is 'well isn't that good enough?' but the reality is that good enough is not good enough. It is good enough for the odd transaction, with the occasional random flirtatious customer, but it is not good enough if you want to build an outstanding business that is profitable and sustainable in the long-term, due to customer retention and referral. Customers know this, they don't have to be trained, and they know exactly what is good for them and where they should spend their money. It is ironic then, that so many businesses fail to grasp some very fundamental principles when it comes to selling.

In my experience nothing should be more complicated than it needs to be and sometimes the very best ideas are those which are put together in the most simple of fashions.

A customer service model

Following is a model that I believe works when it comes to customer service. Customers who contact you will only ever need or want two things:

1. They need a solution to a problem.

2. They want to feel in some way 'special'.

Looking at number one, whether you are a hairdressers, a garage, an electronics manufacturer or you provide research services for off-shore oil companies, you are providing a physical or a psychological solution to somebody's real or imagined problem.

Very often the only time that customers contact an organisation is when they have a problem with something they have purchased. So, for example, if they purchase something by mail order, or buy something from a shop, they will usually only be prompted to call the hotline number, write, or go back into the shop for service when something doesn't meet their expectations, or something goes wrong. Obviously these needs should be put right and the better that they are put right, the more satisfied the customer is going to be. Or are they?

The second element of any customer service satisfaction model is that each and every single customer has to feel in some way special.

EXAMPLE

ONE PARTICULARLY VIVID EXAMPLE is of a large multinational credit card company who suffered a three per cent fall in their credit card attrition in a particular 12-month period. This was probably about five times more than the average should have been and it took the marketing and operations people by surprise. The first thing they did was to look to the competition: which one of their competitors was running a particular promotion to rob them of their customers? However, market surveys and market intelligence found that there were no particularly different or dynamic customer attraction programmes being run by their competitors over the previous few months, certainly nothing that would account for and explain the sudden drop in current credit card renewals. So they began to phone some of their customers and ask them why they hadn't renewed their credit card and continued with them. The answers varied, but there was one particular trend coming out: 'you don't make us feel special anymore'. The fact is that one of the reasons that people held this particular credit card and paid a premium for doing so, over and above normal credit cards, was that they felt special using it.

The second thing that influenced customers was that when they phoned up and used the information and travel booking services that the company offered to its better customers, the actual quality of the response was not very good. Basic information was not known and simple questions had to be asked again and again before operators began to understand what the customer was looking for. Not knowing answers to questions such as: 'Where is JFK airport?' – did not go down well to a seasoned traveller who expected a travel operator to know the answer. The company set about beginning to reverse these feelings of unspecialness that customers were experiencing. It wasn't that there was anything particularly bad that customers could mention but there was nothing, either, particularly good. Comments such as: 'we just feel like we're being processed not served' were quite common.

Following are what I would consider to be the seven most important elements in making a customer feel special, over and above solving their initial problem or basic concern. By some strange coincidence, when put together these seven elements will actually spell the word 'special':

1. Speed and time

2. Personal interaction with a customer

3. Expectations

4. Courtesy and competence

5. Information and keeping the customer informed

6. Attitude and customer liaison

7. Long-term relationships

1. Speed and time

Speed and time measures are very important factors to many customers. The speed with which your company or organisation can deliver, whatever it is it provides, can actually gain you competitive advantage and allow you to offer higher satisfaction, and maybe even demand, or ask a price premium from your customers for that convenience of doing things faster or quicker. However it is not just about the core product, it is also about every single contact or initiation with a customer, from answering the telephone, to replying to letters, to the length of a phone call, to how long you've been put on hold etc. The customer measures all these factors, largely unconsciously.

EXAMPLES

A MORTGAGE AND LOAN provider can actually increase not only their sales, but also customer satisfaction, by putting a speed programme into their operations. Reducing the time it takes from the first enquiry to the customer receiving the loan is an obvious benefit to both the customer and the company. Many companies now, from the point of enquiry, can actually go through the process of vetting, authorisation and actually allocating the money to an account within 24 hours, something that was considered impossible even only a few years ago. In some cases some organisations can give you a mortgage on a property within a matter of days, if you go in with a valuation and evidence of your pay etc.

On the other hand let's take a minor issue: a call centre will know that the percentage number of calls that hang up increases dramatically as the length of time on hold increases. It may be that after a certain time – say a minute or two – there are very few calls left at all. If your call centre or your telephone inbound operation is a sales line, then this is costing you a fortune in terms of lost revenue. If your operation is a customer support operation then this delay in responding to the telephone can be costing you thousands of pounds in lost customer revenue; not to mention increased aggravation when they actually do get through.

ANOTHER EXAMPLE THAT HIGHLIGHTS perhaps the increasing importance of speed to our society is a lift manufacturer, who in designing the lifts for a large public building initiated some customer research. The research, through secret cameras and discussions groups, showed that the things that matter most to customers, when it comes to speed in a lift, were how quickly the doors close, the speed with which the lift begins to move after pressing the floor button and how quickly the lights appear when your waiting for the lift on a floor. The actual speed of the lift moving from floor to floor is largely irrelevant, it would appear, to many customers. A simple device that lift manufacturers have used for years to actually make the lift appear to move faster is to put mirrors on the inside of the lift, commonly thought to be an antidote to any slight claustrophobia that might be experienced. They are, in fact, a good visual distraction so that the mind does not notice the extra few seconds a low powered lift may be taking.

2. Personal interaction with a customer

How well and how able an organisation does this varies from the small to the large. For example: small details matter – remembering a customer's name, a tone of voice and remembering details about that customer.

EXAMPLES

A LARGE CHAIN OF bars and pubs in London trains its staff on memory techniques. Once trained they can remember 300 individuals by face and all the details pertinent to their business and possibly social life, so that when somebody comes into the bar they can chat to them knowledgeably, they remember them and they come back again and again. In the same way, if you have a complex inquiry with an insurance company or a computer supplier and the problem takes several telephone calls or letters to actually resolve the problem, you don't want to have to keep repeating all of the information. A point of contact computer system can capture all the details of the interaction and therefore make the customer feel much more special. Personalised mail shots, newsletters, magazines that contain articles personalised to different types of reader, or indeed each and every reader, are very important.

A MAJOR OFFICE SUPPLIES company actually prints the most popular items ordered by each customer on the front page of every catalogue at a price and a discount which is unique to that customer because of their previous buying pattern. It is increasingly common and possible with technology, to create products and services uniquely for each and every customer. It may not be long before each and every one of us will buy a suit or a car or a computer, which is unique and personally designed – made to measure – for our requirements. The age of the mass-market product is fast disappearing.

A SPECIALIST MOUNTAIN BIKE manufacturer no longer provides standard models to shops for customers to buy; instead they produce prototypes for demonstration purposes. The bike that you choose will be designed on computer, then downloaded digitally to the factory, where it will be assembled precisely to your requirements, including colour and stickers, and then delivered to your home. It is actually cheaper for the organisation to do this and it is also faster to build.

Go through your entire organisation and identify every opportunity that you possibly can to make the customer feel unique and an individual. Train people that answer the telephone and deal with customers face-to-face, to treat every single customer as, not their only customer, but their most important customer.

3. Expectations

The ability to manage expectations well and then systematically and consistently exceed them is the hallmark of a successful business. There are only three kinds of physical and emotional states that you can leave your customer in:

A delighted happy customer

As Tom Peters calls it: 'A customer that goes 'wow' when they deal with your organisation'. This kind of customer will come back to you, will tell their friends about their experience and will become an advocate for your business – an unpaid salesperson. The way that you attract this kind of feeling is to exceed, deliberately and consciously, their expectations. It is to try and find something extra to do that they don't anticipate, and to surprise them with something that makes them smile. In many cases this is not that difficult to do. If you take the principle that little things matter most to customers, then it is only a matter of creativity, not budget, that can create the differences that make a difference to the customer's experience.

A satisfied customer

On the other hand, a satisfied customer is a customer whose expectation is actually equal to their experience. It is not any better significantly, neither is it any worse – they are satisfied. However, this does not seem to enter the customer's memory for any long period of time. Neither does it move them, necessarily, to return or to recommend. Your only hope if you deliver satisfactory service is that your competitors are in some way far worse than you are.

A dissatisfied customer

This may be frustration, annoyance or impatience. It is simply defined where the experience of what you get as a customer is less than your expectation. Many organisations are actually saved from extinction and possible ruin because they have such low expectations within their customers that their experience, whilst falling below many other standards, manages to escape dissatisfaction. For example: many trades' people have customers who have a low expectation of the work or punctuality that they may offer. When they find a tradesman that can offer them quality work – on time, to schedule and to budget, (which are not normally outstanding qualities) – it is because of their low expectations of the work.

Applying this process of managing and then exceeding expectation is one that can happen randomly and through the creative ingenuity of a few customer-focused individuals, but it really shouldn't be left to chance. The most important point to remember is to always under promise and over deliver. Many businesses today strive to win customers by telling them things they think they would like to hear and by sounding impressive in their sales and marketing pitches, brochures and presentations. This over promising has poor experience and poor customer satisfaction built into it – it is doomed to fail. It will consign your organisation to living forever as a hit-and-run customer business – a smash and grab when it comes to customers.

EXAMPLE

A MAJOR VIDEO EQUIPMENT manufacturer that supplies high value and sophisticated equipment to television studios and editing suites was experiencing terrible levels of customer satisfaction. Due to the complexity and the uniqueness of the customisation that had to go in to building recording and editing desks, delays were often incurred. This would mean that customer deadlines or customer projects would sometimes be four or six, or even more weeks, beyond what they expected to be the date of installation. The company had many reasons for this. For example, many of the products had to be sourced from Japan and this took time to actually ship and move through customs. Once in the UK the system desks had to be built, software programmed in, tested and then installed on the customer's site. Constant revisions of hardware and software meant that there were often incompatibilities and system errors when none were anticipated (even though they should have been). After a lengthy process of investigating the order processing, the technical support and systems testing it became apparent that there was one root cause for the customer dissatisfaction and that dissatisfaction was more serious than first imagined. An increasing number of customers were suing the organisation for late

delivery and in some cases cancelling orders worth hundreds of
thousands of pounds. The root cause of this customer dissatisfaction
was traced back to the sales process. Salespeople, unwittingly and keen
to close business, were quoting delivery times of four to six weeks. In
reality nothing was ever delivered in less than ten weeks.

You may think that it would be possible, once the order was secured,
to actually reset the customer's expectation to ten weeks. You may
also think that this type of capital investment, something a video or
recording company might actually only do for a few weeks a year, may
not be too critical. However, consider for a moment that once you've
placed your order for your new editing suite and desk, you will probably
sell and decommission the existing equipment that you have from the
date that you have been told the new equipment will be installed. You
will then probably book work and take orders from your customers
to do things that you can do on the latest new equipment that you
are buying from this organisation. When non-delivery is then
informed you are faced with having to cancel paid work from some
of your best customers, who in turn will have to go away and tell their
customers that they can't deliver what they'd promised. So it all begins
to get rather messy. Why? Simply because somebody didn't under
promise and over deliver. If it is mentioned early enough in the sales
process and enough is done at the time, then the customers will
overcome and live with longer lead times and at least they'll have a
choice. So always make sure that you and your organisation deliver
more than you promise.

As somebody once said to me on a train: 'All the trains and the timeta-
bles these days – if you add the minutes up, are scheduled to go slower
and take longer than they did ten years ago'. In actual fact the reverse
should be true. However, train companies understand that nobody
ever measures how long a journey takes in minutes – they only notice
what time the train arrives, compared to the time that it was supposed
to arrive.

Make sure that all the expectations you ever set for your customers are clear and specific, no more vague 'as soon as possible', or 'it should be there in a few days'. Manage the customer's expectation and build a buffer of, say, at least 50 per cent, into all time deadlines. Give the customer a pleasant surprise rather than an annoyance.

4. Courtesy and competence

The two go hand in hand. Statistics show that customers seem to be happier being served by an enthusiastic amateur rather than an indifferent expert. Now for you this might be determined by whatever it is you're being served with as a customer. For example: if I was going to the dentist I think I might put up with some indifference if it was an expert dentist. However, the reality is of course that we want both. I would like a dentist that was relaxed and personable and at the same time accurate with their instruments.

Common courtesies and manners are very important, probably more important than you may consider at this point. They are also, very often, culturally based – for example: German consumers will place less importance than Italian or British consumers on such things as friendliness and personality. How you can actually be courteous and good mannered will also vary, for example, in Britain many people will shy away from the perhaps over zealous American style of being best buddies and will avoid expressions such as 'have a nice day' even though, when said sincerely, customers warm to them.

Competence means that whoever serves the customer in your business or whoever supports people that serve customers in your business has to do things and do them well. It means getting things right first time. It means knowing what you should know. It means doing what you can do to the best that you can do it – competence and courtesy, hand in hand – it's a licence to keep customers for life.

5. Information and keeping the customer informed

As mentioned earlier, the world today is a much more complicated place than in the past. Technology, social changes and education patterns have created a mass of information. For example, this book will be one of thousands of books that are printed on this topic every single year. Trying to find something on the Internet, in a library, in a newspaper or in a magazine becomes an impossible task. As John Naisbit once said: 'We are drowning in information and starving for knowledge'.

One of the simplest ways to keep customers feeling special and make them feel important to you and your organisation is to keep them informed. Keep them informed of things they're waiting for and let them know how things are going. If there's an expectation that's going to be broken or damaged then let them know as soon as you know – they will almost certainly forgive you if you do this sincerely. But if you don't they probably never will.

For example: have you ever waited at home for an engineer or a home delivery? Just the fact that they couldn't give you a time is annoying enough but then when they don't turn up, having you or somebody else waiting in for most of the day is very frustrating. Interestingly enough some companies can actually give you a time as to when somebody will be in your home within 20 minutes – why can't everybody do this? If you're in a home delivery business, or any delivery business, then this is something that needs to preoccupy you.

How can you keep customers informed of what it is that you're doing, of your business products and services and of changes? My suggestion is that you look at the customers and then define the best way to inform them. Is it by phone calls, letters, e-mail, magazines, advertising, word of mouth, and posters? Whatever it is that you need to do, do it. But remember to focus on the customer and the information they need and their choice for receiving it.

6. Attitude and customer liaison

Attitude is not always easy to understand, train or instill. So let's look at what sort of attitude we mean. It is generally defined as a positive, enthusiastic and helpful attitude – somebody that seems more alive than dead, it means somebody who seems to enjoy what they do or enjoys dealing with customers, not just somebody who happens to do this as a job to earn a living. Even though this may be true, a good customer service experience is one where the customer service person pretends if nothing else, that they enjoy their job – they like doing what they do and they are pleased to see the customer. If the customer representative can do this, the customer will pretend to enjoy buying from them and pretend enough that they will probably come back.

One of the most important aspects of attitude is when the customer is dissatisfied. The customer will then seem to view life through a telephoto lens and every detail or every aspect of the interaction will come under scrutiny. Therefore, the attitude must be to look at a glass of water as half full, instead of half empty.

One of the most important and outward expressions of attitude is the verbal and non-verbal behaviour that people use at critical times. Simple expressions such as: 'I can't do that' or 'There's nothing I can do' or 'That's our company policy' or 'I only work here' or 'You've come through to the wrong extension', only frustrate the customer. Some of these factors, of course, may not be because of anything the person can do; however, it is their attitude that will often create more of an annoyance with the customer than the policy itself. A simple solution to this is that whenever somebody has to be told they can't do something, within the same sentence they have to know what they can do or may do. So, for example: 'I can't deal with this myself but what I can do is take your name and number and have somebody call you back within the hour'. This will not solve the problem immediately but it will make the customer feel special.

The attitude that will work, if you can instill it, is that every single customer is your most important customer. Instead of seeing a customer for the transaction value that they spend at that time or for the nature of their enquiry, see the customer as a million pound customer, somebody who has access to a large revenue, either through their direct spending or indirectly through referrals and repeat business.

7. Long-term relationships

This is the final element of making a customer feel special. A customer will feel special if the organisation that they've dealt with once or just a few times will actually reward, recognise and encourage their loyalty. This will not work with every customer and some customers are rampantly and consistently disloyal. However, for the majority of customers, either business or personal, given the right elements and environment they would prefer to be consistent. Indeed many people think that the drive for consistency in sameness is one of the strongest human instincts of all, perhaps more so than survival. This explains why so many companies and organisations that offer seemingly poor service and low levels of customer satisfaction seem to survive. It is because they exploit the customer's consistency drive and often customers will rationalise to themselves: 'It's better the devil you know than the devil you don't know' – i.e. everyone's probably just as bad, we might as well stick with these people because we know just how bad they are.

So right from the start, maybe from the first sales enquiry, right the way through until the customer's been trading with you for many years, always think about what else you can do to serve them. What other products and services can you sell them? Even simple expressions at the end of a phone call such as: 'Is there anything else I can help you with?' or 'Please give me a call back if you have anymore questions', right the way through to letting the customer know what else you can do to help them. With the advent of the Internet and e-commerce this becomes even more simple, for example, searching on a book site for a particular title will probably bring up the title you're looking for, but also, the screen will probably suggest other titles that people who have bought that book have also purchased.

So you may find other things of interest to you. This can then be put into a process of informing you when books are released that could be of interest to you, because they fit whatever you looked for in the past. This technology exists now, it doesn't have to be limited to the Internet – you could be running this on the back of your sales ledger, you could be looking at companies in terms of acquiring products and services or building partnerships with other organisations that offer your customers higher levels of satisfaction, presumably at a profit to yourselves as well.

When put together each one of these seven elements will accelerate customer satisfaction beyond even their wildest dreams. They need to become a constant preoccupation to the customer-focused business. A constant level of paranoia needs to be installed at every level of management: 'Are we doing things quickly enough?' 'Are we personalising and treating customers as individuals?' 'Are we managing, exceeding and delivering extra customer experiences?' 'How competent and courteous are all our staff when it comes to dealing with customers – from the humblest van driver to our PR manager dealing with the world's press?' 'How well do we keep our customers and our customer groups informed, right down from the instructions we give them on the back of a packet, through to the information they need when they are solving a problem?' 'What is the attitude of our people – how is this attitude perceived?' The only real measure is that which customers deduce. And then 'how well do we actually look to encourage long-term customer relationships?'

If you can begin to implement ideas based around these seven elements and make them a constant focus of attention, you will become unerringly more customer-focused and your customers will become increasingly more loyal and profitable. A customer that feels special will spend more, ask any successful restaurant or hotel.

chapter five **Achieving service excellence**

Introduction

Customer focus is the ability to provide predictably positive experiences that consistently meet or exceed your customers' expectations. This chapter will show you how to provide these experiences for your customers. You will learn about your customers' expectations and about what you must do to meet or exceed them. You will gain not only a deeper understanding of the value you bring to your customers, but also a new confidence in your ability to retain those customers, by providing a service of consistent high quality.

Customer focus should be managed by 'moments of truth'. A 'moment of truth' refers to 'any episode when a customer comes into contact with any aspect of your business and, on the basis of that contact, forms an opinion about the quality of your service and the quality of your product'. A good customer-focused organisation will try and create more moments of truth, not less. They will try and increase the number of contacts and the frequency of contacts that a customer has with an organisation, whether it is looking at a brochure, speaking on the phone, reading an e-mail or clicking on a web site etc. These moments of truth need to be encouraged and maximised.

It is every customer-focused company's aspiration to manage every 'moment of truth' to the best possible outcome for the customer. Every customer contact is a 'moment of truth', an opportunity to delight or disappoint. The skills you will learn in this chapter will help you to manage each of your everyday 'moments of truth' to help to build lifelong customer relationships.

Exercise: The customer experience

1. Think about a personal experience in which you were treated very well as a customer. Write three words or phrases to describe your feelings in that experience.

2. Think about a personal experience in which you were treated poorly as a customer. Write three words or phrases to describe what you wanted to do in response to that poor treatment.

The customer interaction cycle

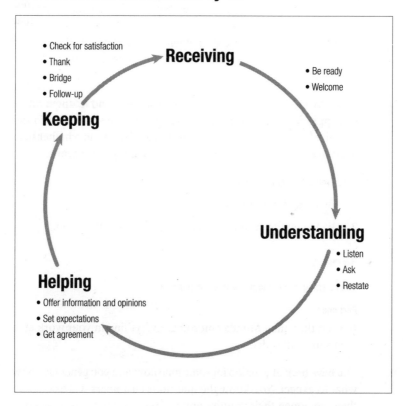

Figure 3: The customer interaction cycle

Figure three shows a cycle – the customer interaction cycle. There are four basic elements to the cycle:

1. Receiving
2. Understanding
3. Helping
4. Keeping.

Receiving

As a customer, you often know within the first few moments of a visit or call to a company or to a colleague, whether you are glad you made the visit or call and whether you will be provided with good service. These first impressions frequently depend on how you are received.

As a provider, you want to welcome customers and let them know you appreciate their business and their input – they are a valued individual. How the customer is received may determine whether they want to continue to do business with you and your organisation.

You need to do two things:

1. Be ready for almost any eventuality
2. Welcome the customer – make a good first impression.

Be ready

One morning in a customer support department

Part one

It is a rather quiet Monday morning. Everything in your work area seems to be in order.

You have been at your job for some time now, and you generally know what to expect. You know the questions customers will ask before they even open their mouths, and usually you know the answers.

Today you feel quite ready to handle any tough problem or challenging customer who might come along. 'Emotionally prepared' is how you describe yourself. As you scan your work area, you say to yourself, 'This is too good to be true. Any minute now it'll get busy. But I'm ready'.

Pouring yourself a cup of coffee, you settle into your chair and begin to look through the mail in your in-box, and then...

Part two

Within minutes your calm, quiet morning erupts into a blaze of activity:

The telephone rings. It is a colleague who wants to transfer a call from a customer who has been having problems with his invoicing. Able as you are to answer virtually any billing question, you accept the call, only to discover that the customer's account is handled by another office, not your own. You cannot answer the customer's question, and he is irate at having been transferred twice already.

While you are on the phone with him, another colleague rushes in to pick up a report he left in your in-box last week. You glanced at it briefly on Friday and noted that it required your review and input, but, since it was not due back until today, you put it aside. Your colleague now tells you that your manager needs the report back for a presentation this afternoon. Rolling your eyes as the customer on the telephone continues to complain, you point your colleague to a chair and begin to shuffle through your in-box in search of the report.

The other telephone line starts ringing. No one else in your area is picking up the call, so you put the irate customer on hold and pick up the new call yourself. It is a regular customer looking to verify some status information quickly. Turning to your computer screen to access her information, you find a blinking message that tells you the network has been down for the past 15 minutes.

As you apologise to the customer and explain that you are unable to access the information she needs, you notice that the other, irate customer has hung up and that your colleague is halfway down the hall on his way to your manager's office with the unreviewed report in his hand.

Welcome: how it looks and sounds

Welcoming a customer takes about 30 seconds. To deliver a truly effective welcoming statement, however, each of the following must consistently convey that you are ready and willing to focus on the customer:

Tone of voice

The tone of voice you use with customers often says more to them than you might expect. Tone of voice is like a radio transmitting subtle sound waves. Customers receive these subtle signals, which tell them how you really feel about what you are doing. Our attitude is conveyed through our voice. Aspects of voice tone include:

▶ **Volume** – soft or loud

▶ **Fluctuation** – varied or monotonous

▶ **Clarity** – clear or muffled

▶ **Rate of speech** – rapid or slow

▶ **Emotion** – hostile or pleasant.

Verbal language

Language is a verbal expression. It is what you use to introduce and to greet customers. In the brief welcoming phase, customers form opinions of you, in part from the words you use. Aspects of verbal language include:

▶ **Attitude** – courteous or uninterested

▶ **Effectiveness** – clear or encumbered by jargon

▶ **Appropriateness** – short-spoken or long-winded.

Body language

This includes posture, gestures, and facial expressions; like tone of voice, it communicates attitude. Physical behaviours signal to customers how you really feel about them and about what you are doing. Body language can even be communicated over the telephone; when you smile, people can sense it. Aspects of body language include:

▶ **Presence** – energetic or apathetic

▶ **Eye contact** – direct or evasive

▶ **Spatial proximity** – close or distant

▶ **Facial expression** – smiling or lifeless.

Another truism that is worth remembering at this point is that customers remember and notice everything – either consciously or unconsciously. For example, walking into a garage service reception, an airport waiting lounge, sitting on a plane – customers will notice tatty, fraying seat covers, stains on table tops, litter in the corner, dust on telephones, scruffiness, poor body odour, rudeness, lack of eye contact – all these things go noticed by customers. However, they often go unnoticed by the organisation that commits such sins.

ACTION PLAN: RECEIVING

Be ready

Of the three kinds of customer needs associated with being ready, which one are you best prepared to meet on a daily basis? Why?

☐ Informational   ☐ Physical   ☐ Emotional

Which of the three customer needs do you most need to improve your ability to meet, in order to serve your customers? Why?

☐ Informational   ☐ Physical   ☐ Emotional

Welcome

What can you do differently or better to improve the way you welcome your customers?

Understanding

Once the customer has been greeted and acknowledged, the next stage is to move into a process of understanding what the nature of their enquiry is.

This is often the most difficult stage, as you have to concentrate completely on what the customer is saying. It can be particularly hard to stay focused on your customers when they call or stop by your office with the same questions and requests day after day. Yet customers value highly the personalised attention you can give. A provider who focuses on the customer at this stage concentrates on everything the customer is saying – not only the words themselves, but also the way they are spoken – and responds in a way that shows appreciation of, and concern for, the customer's feelings and needs.

The emphasis in this stage is on identifying your customers' needs and expectations exactly. In routine situations, you may find that this requires only a brief conversation. At other times (for example, when your customer is unsure about what he or she needs or when the situation is complex), you may need to spend more time to make sure that you understand clearly. In either situation, you must focus on the customer as an individual.

Whether it is a sales enquiry or a customer support issue, the skills you need to understand your customers are:

► Listening for feelings and facts

► Asking questions to clarify

► Restating feelings and facts.

Listening to the feelings and facts, as stated by customers, is critical to maintaining a positive interaction and building trust and confidence. It requires a great deal of concentration, especially when the customer is difficult or upset.

How much you use the other skills – asking and restating – depends on the complexity of the customer's requests and whether he or she is difficult or upset. For example, if you are performing a routine task for a customer, you probably ask only a limited number of questions and the conversation is usually brief. But if you are trying to understand the needs of a customer who is confused about your organisation's products or services, you ask many questions and restate what he or she has said to make sure that you have heard all of the information accurately.

Even when you are certain that you understand, it is critical to restate, so customers know you understand. Empathise with their point of view; then restate to show and assure them that indeed you do understand what they need and why it is important to them.

Asking effective questions

The information you receive from customers is only as good as the questions you ask them. The key is knowing how to construct questions that will uncover important information about customers' needs. There are three kinds of questions; each designed to obtain specific types of information from customers:

Closed questions

▶   Are used to obtain or confirm specific facts. They are mostly used in fast-moving, uncomplicated interactions with customers and elicit brief responses:

'When would you like it delivered?'

'Do you know who your consultant is?'

'Was the number easy to find?'

'When do you need it?'

▶   They usually begin with *is, do, can, how many,* or *who.*

Open-ended questions

▶   Are used to elicit more information from the customer. They are mainly used in complex situations, in which the customer's need may be unclear, or in which many choices are available:

'What kind of service are you looking for?'

'How can I help you with those applications?'

'When does the problem occur?'

'How do you use the report?'

► They usually begin with *who, what, how, when, where,* or *why.*

High-gain questions

► Are open-ended questions that encourage the customer to evaluate, analyse, speculate, or express feelings.

'What are the three most important things I could do to work with you on this installation?'

'How would you compare our service with that of other suppliers?'

'How would you like us to resolve this situation?'

'Of the information you receive from me, what is most valuable?'

► They usually begin with *what, if, suppose,* or *how.*

Restating feelings and facts

This involves showing customers that you have heard them and that you understand their situation and their priorities. Using a tone of voice that conveys empathy, restate the customer's feelings first, and then fix the problem:

► Identify the customer's feelings and the facts

► Acknowledge the customer's feelings

► Summarise the facts.

ACTION PLANNING: UNDERSTANDING

Listen

What are the biggest challenges in listening to your customers? What skills can you use to listen more effectively?

Ask

Write two questions you could ask of your most important customers. Focus your questions on uncovering more information about your customers' needs, their level of satisfaction with your organisation's products or services, or other areas that are important to them.

Restate

Think of a recent experience in which your customers had strong feelings. How might you have restated the feelings to show that you understood?

Think of a recent experience in which the facts were complicated or a request was ambiguous. How might you have restated the facts to show that you understood?

Helping

The third stage of the cycle is helping. Helping might simply be explaining something or giving some information. It may be discussing various options that will solve the customer's need or enquiry. Instead of saying one thing, it will almost certainly be more persuasive and more satisfactory, from the customer's experience, to have a small number of options presented. It also means getting agreement and setting expectations, it doesn't mean saying whatever it is the customer wants to hear or suggesting vague or exaggerated expectations.

To guarantee that customers get not only what they ask for, but also what they really want, you need to apply some helping skills:

▶   Offer information and options

▶   Set realistic expectations

▶   Get agreement on the course of action.

To focus on the customer at this stage is to ensure they make the right choice for their own situation. Service providers who genuinely focus on the customer show a sincere desire to help – even when the situation is difficult.

Helping gives you an opportunity to meet the customer's needs and to create a satisfied customer for your organisation. Have you ever received exactly what you had asked for and not been satisfied? Customers frequently find themselves in such a situation. There are several reasons why it can happen.

For instance, the customer might not have known that other options were available. An office manager ordered 300 network printers in a certain configuration, unaware that she might have ordered the printers configured in a different way to serve more users. She learned about the other option only after the printers had been installed.

The customer might not have known what to expect – such as the man who ordered a new laptop to use on a business trip the following week, unaware that it would take three weeks for the laptop to be delivered to him.

Or the customer might not have agreed to specific details. Imagine that a customer and a service provider had discussed two contracts extensively. The customer selected one contract form, but later was surprised to learn that a clause he had wanted was missing from it. The service provider had not obtained the customer's agreement on the specific details of the contract the customer had selected.

It is the service provider's responsibility to share all appropriate information, to give the customer as much choice as possible, to set the customer's expectations, and to get agreement on the course of action. The key thing is that the customer should never need to pull information from the service provider.

Offering options and setting expectations

Research has shown that customers like options. They like to have a choice in how their needs will be addressed. Offering information and options is a way to educate customers and involve them in selecting the solution that best meets their particular situation.

As you use the skills of offering information and options and setting expectations, consider the factors and the customer's requirements and priorities. These factors help you group or prioritise what matters most to your customer, and thus provide options that meet the customer's expectations.

Note the relevant information you need and be knowledgeable about your organisation's products or services (policies, procedures, standards etc). You must provide reliable information to the customer.

Put yourself in the customer's place as you generate options involving your organisation's products or services. Your colleagues or your manager can help you develop options beyond the obvious ones. Sometimes what appears at face value to be foolish actually works! Determine which options best meet the customer's needs, in light of the data you have gathered about the customer and your organisation.

Identify what you can and cannot do to satisfy the customer. Consider any constraints that may be relevant. This minimises the risk of a gap forming between what the customer expects and what you can deliver. Research shows that high-performing service providers set realistic expectations with customers. As a result, their performance is consistently excellent.

Discuss and select options with customers, so that they can choose what works best for them. Even if the information and options you offer are straightforward, relate your responses to the customers' needs, values, and priorities. For example:

'You mentioned that you need the equipment for your presentation on Tuesday. You can have it delivered to you by Monday afternoon.'

The options and expectations worksheet that follows is designed to help you plan for and work through particularly complex or tough customer situations – those in which you need to step back, think through the options, and decide how to set expectations. The worksheet is a visual tool for planning, for consulting with others in your work unit or your manager. It helps you to keep your focus on the customer and to link your solutions to the customer's values; it is not intended for every customer interaction.

The service provider in the sample situation is responsible for scheduling resources. The customer involved needs 600 hours of developer time in the next 30 days. This information is recorded at the top of the worksheet.

1. The first column lists the customer's specific requirements and priorities.

2. The second column shows the relevant information the administrator can provide.

3. In the third column are the options the administrator can offer to address the customer's priorities.

4. At the bottom of the worksheet the administrator has summarised the expectations he or she can set with the customer.

Sample worksheet – options and expectations

Customer: IT applications • **Service provider**: Your organisation's administrator

Customer situation: Needs 600 hours of developer time in the next 30 days

Specific customer requirements/priorities	Information (about your products or services)	Options (to address customer needs)
Project completed in 30 days	Two developers available now	Overtime
	Two developers available in 15 days	Use senior developer to speed delivery
Budget limited	Rates vary	
Technical competence	Developers are competent	
Experienced with customer business applications	Two available developers have experience	Train non-experienced developers
	Two developers available in 15 days have limited experience	

Expectations to set with your customer

What you can do	What you cannot do
Provide 480 hours in 30 days	Provide 600 hours of experienced development time for 30 days, except by using overtime
Provide senior developer at start-up to provide design guidance	
Have senior developer commit ten hours to advise	

ACTION PLAN: HELPING

▶ What are the most commonly asked questions or queries from customers? Identify these and prepare clear and effective answers in anticipation.

▶ Make sure that all customer services staff have information sources to hand.

▶ Review basic knowledge. How well do people know what they should and can they explain it clearly?

▶ How well do you offer options? Be ready to offer alternatives at each decision point in a customer interaction.

▶ How well can you manage expectations – can't do and can dos? Make a list of ten examples.

Keeping

The final stage in the customer interaction cycle is keeping the customer informed and satisfied. Customers vividly remember first and last impressions. Once the customer has been helped you then need to check their level of satisfaction, thank them for their time, their business and their custom, and bridge to any other aspect that you'd like to mention, or link into some other product information, and ask them if there's anything else that you can help them with. Don't make the simple transaction – the personal transaction – end with whatever they phoned up about and then if there's a follow-up involved, make sure this happens accurately and quickly. The follow-up may only be internal – updating the customer's records, putting in place something that you promised to do or passing on a message – but make sure it is done in a timely and a competent fashion.

The skills involved are:

▶ Check for satisfaction

▶ Thank them for their time

▶ Bridge to other aspects

▶ Follow-up.

Keeping skills are critically important to your relationship with customers. Your ability to conclude interactions with a focus on the future and on continuous improvement, will determine overall how willing customers will be to work with you or your organisation in the future.

You play an important role in creating customer loyalty and in retaining customers. Without you and your work, your organisation could not meet its customers' needs. By keeping your focus on the customer at every stage of the cycle, you consistently communicate that they are valued. The result is customers who wish to continue doing business with you in the future.

ACTION PLANNING: KEEPING

Consider your own work situation. Which of the keeping skills will you want to focus on in your work with customers? How will you focus on these skills?

Example

No matter what business you're in – whether you're a car service garage, a microelectronics manufacturer, a specialist graphics designer, a marketing consultant, an advertising agency, a Harley Street specialist or you manage a large public building or utility – whatever it happens to be, don't measure yourself against the other people in your industry. When it comes to creating moments of truth, measure yourself against the best examples you can find and if you can't define them, then create them.

One of the developments that have shaken the airline industry in Europe is the rise of low cost airlines. Interestingly these airlines, whilst charging a fraction of the price of the more well established major airlines, are actually able to offer better punctuality, more comfort, more flexible flight times and service standards of their staff and environment in excess of and exceeding the experience of the passengers of the other established airlines. They looked at their business and said 'how can we do it even better'? Just because we are going to charge people half the fare, they should not have to experience half the standard or service. The staff are cheerful and they're bright and the check-in times are a fraction of the time it takes for other airlines charging far more.

Your goal is to create true moments of truth that stand out in the customer's mind. Interestingly enough, if your product or service is of a lower value than some of your competitors and you can offer a higher level of customer experience you will, of course, stand out more than the other way round. And it needn't cost you anymore. You don't pay for quality; you pay for the lack of it.

Partner exercise – process mapping

It is important to review how well your processes really serve customer's needs and expectations, carry out the following exercise with your team or colleagues.

In this exercise you focus on a work process that is important to you and your customers. You create a map of the current process and the flow of tasks involved. Doing so improves your use of teamwork to meet customers' expectations.

Step 1

Individually, follow the guidelines below and create a map of the process you selected. Consider your main responsibilities and select a process that involves teamwork with other departments.

Process mapping guidelines

▶ Identify the key process that is affecting your customer.

▶ Map the way the current process works.

▶ Identify the major departments or functions involved in the process and write them on the left-hand side of the process map.

▶ Identify the major tasks or activities involved and place them in the proper sequence from left to right in the row of the appropriate department. Time of activities or tasks flows horizontally from left to right.

▶ Connect each activity to the next one in the sequence with an arrow. The next activity may be either within or outside of the function of the last one.

Step 2

Respond to the questions on the process mapping worksheet.

Step 3

With your partner, review the process and your observations. Spend 20 minutes on this. Consider how you might improve the process. What help or support will you need in advancing your ideas for improvement?

Summary: teamwork

▶ Use the customer interaction cycle to ensure smooth handoffs.

▶ Share responsibility for results.

▶ Review workflow to improve handoffs.

Handling challenging situations

Challenging situations are critical moments during which customers can be satisfied or lost forever. When you handle dissatisfied customers well, you help retain business and customer goodwill; a successful recovery can even help build customer loyalty. It is important to be focused, personable, and sincere. Keep in mind that a customer's strong language or angry words are not intended as a personal attack.

Using the customer interaction cycle

Customers may come to you already upset, or they can become dissatisfied at any stage of the interaction cycle. Dealing with challenging situations requires the use of the customer interaction cycle in its entirety, to turn dissatisfied customers into satisfied customers. Particular emphasis should be put on the understanding and helping stages.

Receiving

Begin by receiving customers in a way that communicates a positive attitude through verbal and non-verbal language.

Be ready

Prepare yourself mentally to be calm, professional, and empathetic – even in a tough situation.

Take a few minutes to separate yourself emotionally from your job. Think of yourself as 'playing a role' to help you avoid taking customer complaints personally; they are directed at your role, not you.

Welcome

Show by your words and manner that you intend to be responsive. Resist the urge to be defensive or aloof.

Understanding

This is probably the most critical stage for dealing with dissatisfied customers. The rule of thumb is, 'focus on the customer first, then focus on the problem'. Use your understanding skills: listen, then restate and ask questions.

Listen

Listen first and encourage customers to talk. Use phrases such as 'I see' and 'Tell me more'. The ability to recover well depends on you putting your own emotions aside and listening actively to customers. It is critical to listen for feelings, facts, missed expectations, and urgency.

▶ Do not defend yourself.

▶ Do not try to solve the problem immediately.

▶ When in doubt, ask customers to elaborate.

▶ Throughout the process of handling challenging situations, continue to listen actively.

Ask questions

After listening and asking customers to elaborate, ask questions to clarify the complaint, discover specific concerns and draw out any underlying concerns. Encourage customers to elaborate and keep them involved.

Be careful about asking too many questions. Prolonged questioning can feel like a cross-examination and can irritate an already aggravated customer.

Restate feelings and facts

After you have asked the questions, listen to the answers and restate to check your understanding of the problem before trying to solve it. Acknowledge the customer's right to be concerned, and indicate your willingness to let them express their point of view completely. Show empathy. Understand how the customer feels by putting yourself in their place. This defuses antagonism and resistance, and helps turn the situation from confrontation to mutual problem solving.

Let the customer know that you understand both the feelings and facts of what they are telling you. Restating these gives you a chance to think about the best way to resolve their problems before you respond with solutions and gives the customer a chance to reassess their position.

Imagine a customer who expected data to be processed in time for inclusion in a special report. You might say:

'You're upset about not having the data ready, and I would be, too (feelings). I understand how important the schedule is and how much work is already done on the report. I'll do my best to help straighten out the problem (feelings). You need the data on an Excel spreadsheet (facts)?'

As part of a recovery strategy, be sure to apologise.

Offer information and options

Having uncovered the nature of the problem, you are ready to respond. The information and options you offer will depend on the nature of the problem:

▶   For misconceptions, offer clarifying details
▶   For complaints, offer a plan of action to respond to them.

If a customer is dissatisfied with all the options you are offering, consult with your manager or colleagues to develop more options. Do it quickly to show a desire to solve the problem.

Set realistic expectations

This is very important in avoiding further problems. Often the problem is the result of a customer having received something other than what they were expecting.

▶ Focus on the positive.

▶ Be specific. Make sure the customer understands what will happen, when, where, and how. Remember that they have already been disappointed once.

Get agreement

Check to see if the customer's problems or objections have been addressed. Listen for any hint that they are still unhappy. If necessary, return to the understanding stage to explore any additional problems.

Continuing with the data example:

'Several things might have happened here. The problem could be with the process of collecting the data, or with the formatting (offering information). I don't know if we'll be able to get this done today, but we'll do everything we can. I'll call you at noon to give you a status report (setting expectations). How does that sound (getting agreement)?'

Keeping

End the interaction by using keeping skills. You need to make an extra effort to ensure customers will continue doing business with your organisation.

Check for satisfaction

Be explicit. If the customer is unhappy when the interaction ends, you are in danger of losing their business for good. It might be a good idea to make sure they are still satisfied with their whole relationship with your organisation.

Our data example ends: 'we really value your business. Does the plan I suggested satisfy your concerns right now? Is there anything else we can do for you (checking for satisfaction)?'

Thank

Thank the customer when the situation has been difficult.

Bridge

Be creative when bridging and following up with customers who have been dissatisfied.

Follow-up

Ask yourself what you could do to get the customer to want to continue doing business with you. A letter from a senior executive in your organisation might help, or an offer of free services.

Remember...

Give immediate attention

▶ Act quickly.

▶ Communicate your intention to be responsive.

Be neutral not defensive

▶ Stay calm.

▶ Pause; take a deep breath.

▶ Do not take it personally.

▶ Avoid fighting back.

Remain professional

▶ Project confidence and respect for the customer.

▶ Be proactive.

▶ Do not reciprocate with the sort of negative and unproductive behaviours and attitudes the customer might have displayed initially.

Remember

▶ Focus on the customer first, then the problem.

▶ Use the customer interaction cycle.

▶ Empathise.

chapter six Managing for customer satisfaction

Introduction

If you are working in a business that is focused and dedicated to customer satisfaction you cannot manage it in the same way as an ordinary or traditional business – it just doesn't work. Organisations have found this to their cost. Implementing policies without changing the organisation first is self-defeating. The organisation will defeat change as soundly as day follows night. However, if you change the organisation and the way people are managed and led and you have developed the policies; ideas, procedures, standards and systems will evolve rapidly and effectively.

The first major change has to be the ritual burning and demolition of the standard organisation chart. Customers, suppliers and employees cannot be forced to work through traditional top down hierarchical management systems. Not only does it give people the wrong feeling; it actually just doesn't work. It's not that it ever worked particularly well anyway, it was just the thing that everyone used when they put together a large organisation. From what I can see, when they began after the Second World War to build large industrial organisations, the only effective model they seemed to have was the government, the army and the military forces. Therefore, these were used as the template for structuring a commercial organisation. I can see no other similarity other than the fact that they involve large numbers of people hopefully working together. But even if they ever worked in the past, they certainly won't work in the future.

Today's manager has to be much more of a communicator than a dictator. They also have to be much more of a facilitator than a policy determinator. Peoples' aspirations have changed, just as the customers have. They need to be treated in a way that encourages them, empowers them and enthuses them to deliver the best for their customers.

The differences between a traditional manager and a customer-focused manager

Firstly, a traditional manager focuses on current goals. Their time and their energy is preoccupied with a series of probably corporate internally focused objectives – whether this is making a sales target, budget, profitability or some other goal, such as market share. On the other hand a customer-focused manager is led and empowered by a vision. A vision based on quality as well as quantity and results. A vision that inherently has a customer satisfaction measure and a vision that creates a feeling of pride and satisfaction in working in that way.

A traditional manager is largely reactive – making decisions, implementing plans based on the input of those above them, around them or in the external environment. 'If it ain't broke, don't fix it', would be a common maxim. Today's manager is largely proactive – 'If it's not broken, break it', because it's going to be broken very soon. Today's manager doesn't wait for things to need a reason for change; they change things for the sake of it. Whether this is just simply the office layout, the times people take their lunch, company policies, prices, brochures, and markets – everything else has to be a proactive activity today. If you wait for the market to change you will probably always be one step behind. One step behind what the customers need and want and what your competitors are doing.

A traditional manager will often seek, either directly or indirectly, to limit other people's participation. Typically, meetings between managers are excluded from input from other people, or they don't involve other people perhaps as much as they should do – this is never seen as necessary. But today it is essential. Today's manager has to promote involvement; they need opinions, thoughts, ideas, and feedback from all levels within the organisation. The best way of achieving this is by one of two methods. The first is one we could loosely name 'random communication', where just by simply creating the environment where people can mix and mingle, communicate, participate and share, ideas can be distributed. The other way is by doing something slightly more formal, by putting in place a series of waterfalls or communication falls where information and participation flows around the organisation.

Traditional managers will probably reward people based on their qualifications or long service. A more customer-focused manager will reward and recognise people based on their ability to enhance customers and deliver excellence. For example: it is not uncommon for managers to regularly single out for some form of payment, or just simple recognition, those people in a customer service team who have gone beyond the normal levels and delivered something extraordinary during their job. Whether it was staying late sorting out a customer problem, coming up with an idea which helped the business move forward, making big improvements in their own work – these are the things that managers reward.

Another thing that has to change if you are going to move forward and lead successfully in a customer-focused organisation is that you have to let go of solving problems yourself. As Peter Druca said: 'Delegation is both the hardest thing and the most essential thing for any successful manager to do'. This has never been more true. Problem solving cannot take place at management level. It must take place at the level to which the customer can gain most satisfaction – whether this is a refund or some other technical issue. If a problem affects a customer, the people that serve that customer have to be empowered with the skills, the knowledge and the authority, together with a sense of responsibility, to provide the best solutions.

One very successful manager who ran a very effective customer service team had a big sign on their wall, it said: 'You can come in here with any problem at all, so long as you have one idea for a solution'. If any member of staff came in with a customer problem or query without a solution they were sent back out until they could come up with at least one idea. Invariably their idea was the one that was chosen as their idea was the one that would work. If it wasn't the right idea then they would discuss it and together come up with an idea that would work. Over a period of time people realised that they had the capability and ingenuity to solve their own problems and the only reason they came through the manager was because of habit or lack of confidence.

A traditional manager also sees their role as controlling information. They will keep their staff and other people on a 'need to know' basis. This is not how it works. Information should be shared, but not broadcast. A good manager will communicate actively and pro-actively to all concerned. He or she will keep them informed of the information they need to deliver the best possible service to the customer. This means the information is timely, relevant and understood.

Managing in today's environment, with the pressures of working with ever demanding customers, will invariably result in matters of conflict and disagreement. Rather than patching these over, ignoring them, or letting them sort themselves out, as is perhaps more traditionally done by managers, these should now be sought out and moderated to a successful outcome.

Another very important difference if you are to grasp the challenge and opportunity of managing effectively in a customer orientated organisation, is the way that a manager will recognise achievement on a day-to-day basis. Often these achievements will have been recognised either indiscriminately or in rather a formal fashion, perhaps through the process of a quarterly or annual appraisal. Achievements need to be recognised quickly and delivered as close in time to their execution. This has been proven to not only reinforce the behaviour but also to maximise the motivation that can come from an achievement being noticed and recognised. They don't actually have to be formal or cost any money, and they can be as simple as people noticing and saying 'thank you' or 'well done'. In large organisations you may see people wearing different coloured name badges or stars or having different grades against their name. This is as they move through and deliver more quality work, rather than achieving a certain time span of employment.

Most importantly a customer-focused manager 'walks the talk'. He or she must act congruently and with the same values and honesty that they want their staff to deliver to their customers. That means they keep commitments, it means they under promise and over deliver, and they make everyone of their employees feel special and a valuable member of the team. Nobody just does a job and goes home, there is a purpose, a value and a mission.

Researchers have found that there is a very strong and direct correlation between the level of customer service that an organisation or individual can deliver and the way that staff are managed. This is known as the customer employee mirror. The way that you manage an employee is directly mirrored in their attitude and behaviours, very often, to the customer. If somebody offers or is unhappy with low performance they will probably leave and work for an organisation that is more in tune with their way of thinking.

Checklist

Below is a quick checklist of ways that you can improve your management of others to enable you to deliver higher customer satisfaction:

1. **Listen to other people around you**, no matter what their experience or lack of it and listen without judgement – every opinion is a valid one. If you hear two or three ideas together they can often spark a fourth, which you wouldn't have arrived at if you'd heard them with a judgement.

2. **Use praise**. Use praise more frequently and more sincerely than you've ever done in the past. Every night when you go home, if you are a manager or even if you are not, ask yourself 'have I said 'thank you' to three people for three different things today?' If you haven't, it either means one of two things: that nobody that you work with, or for, has actually done anything which is worth saying 'thank you' for, or that they have done things of note but you haven't noticed.

3. **If you can't say something positive, don't say anything**. If you went into a meeting with your manager and they ran through a list of 20 things that they were pleased with and just as you were leaving they delivered one negative criticism, the chances are that this is the one thought that would stay with you, the other 20 would disappear in the length and shadow of the negative criticism. Negative criticism has virtually no practical application. If you have to say something then think it through and put it into a positive context. Remember that people will normally do the best

they can with what they have. If they are not doing the best that they can, then you need to help them to see what can be done and what talents, resources or alternatives exist for them.

4. **Always be seen to be fair and honest**. If there's one thing that can demotivate staff and people around you quicker than almost anything, it is people having favourites.

5. **Share your concerns**. Managing a customer service team, an organisation, or being an entrepreneur is not an easy job. Whilst you need to be decisive and have the confidence and courage that inspires people, there is much to be gained from being open and sharing your own hopes, dreams and concerns. One of the things that people often like in working in a small business, perhaps one which has an entrepreneurial flair to it, is the enthusiasm and the sheer energy that those people can put into their day and they do, every single day. Remind people what you're doing, where you're going and why you do what you do.

6. **Become a teacher**. Instead of finding fault, managing by exception, and pointing out where people are going wrong, become obsessed with helping people become twice as good as they are now. If you manage people, or you aspire to manage or lead people, then your goal should be to make sure that as quickly as possible they can do their job twice as well as they're doing it now, even if it means them being promoted or leaving. There is nothing more satisfying than seeing other people around you do well, especially if you know you've contributed to that. Don't ask yourself 'what can I do for myself'? Instead, ask yourself 'how Can I help my team become a better team'? Take a few minutes at regular intervals, at random times during the day if necessary, and teach people different ways of doing things – upgrade their skills, explain different aspects of the business, formalise it – put together different training programmes so that people, over a period of time, will really move forward in both their skills, their knowledge and their habits.

7. **Kiesin is a Japanese word** that has no equivalent in the English language. It roughly translates as 'constant and never ending improvement'. The Japanese philosophy is to do a thousand things one per cent better not one thing a thousand per cent better. This means that everybody that you work with – every supplier, every employee, and every manager, everybody in the customer satisfaction value chain – should be constantly required to innovate, to improve and suggest ideas. Coming up with ways to improve how things are done, should almost become a mandatory part of any job.

8. **Develop yourself**. If there's one way that you can get other people to become more interested and more focused on improving themselves, it is to lead by example. Take time out to go on training courses, even though you may be too busy. Take time to read useful information, not just novels, books or newspapers but actual up-to-date books and texts from the experts within your industry. Practise your skills, use them and make sure that they're developed as far as they possibly can be. If it means learning a new language or learning a skill that you don't have then take on that challenge. It is very difficult to manage people well if you have low self-esteem, but if you feel good about yourself and you have that feeling of progress and achievement, then it is very hard for this not to rub off on other people.

9. **Only do the most important things**. Ask yourself that question or a version of it every single minute of the day: 'Is what I'm doing now helping directly or indirectly to increase the number and quality of the customers our organisation has?' Because if it doesn't affect the customer, it shouldn't be done.

chapter seven Customer-focused selling and marketing skills

Introduction

This chapter highlights the most important elements used to achieve a higher level of customer spend, loyalty and quality experience. There are some similarities with existing sales approaches and perhaps most importantly, some differences from conventional selling. As an overview, these are:

Traditional style	Customer-focused
Focus on the product feature and benefits	Focus on the customer
Assume trust and credibility through style not substance	Earn the right and use capability statements to differentiate effectively
Focus on 'winning' sales	Focus on helping customers make buying decisions
Tell the customer of the product or solution features and benefits	Persuade through involvement
Use open and perhaps need-probing questions	Use high-gain questions
Identify service-level needs and opportunities	Probe to develop consequences and pay-offs
Identify simple or immediate needs and opportunities	Target and prioritise potential customers early and maintain contact on a planned basis
Present a single or 'most-favoured' solution	Involve the customer in reviewing 'options'

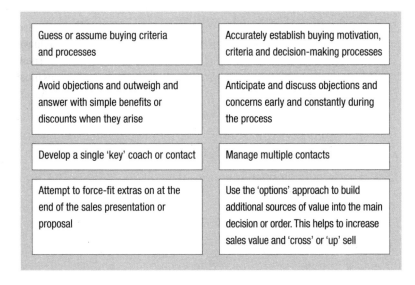

Guess or assume buying criteria and processes	Accurately establish buying motivation, criteria and decision-making processes
Avoid objections and outweigh and answer with simple benefits or discounts when they arise	Anticipate and discuss objections and concerns early and constantly during the process
Develop a single 'key' coach or contact	Manage multiple contacts
Attempt to force-fit extras on at the end of the sales presentation or proposal	Use the 'options' approach to build additional sources of value into the main decision or order. This helps to increase sales value and 'cross' or 'up' sell

Figure 4: Sales and marketing methods

It is likely that each reader will use varying sales and marketing methods – from face-to-face to e-commerce, direct marketing, telephone sales, retail etc. It is possible to adapt and adopt the principles and practices covered here for each and every type of sales and marketing situation. Indeed, you may find yourself recognising examples without having to look too hard or too far. You may also notice the lack of them in companies that you have had a less than positive buying experience with.

Golden chain

One of the most important differences is that today's new customers must be seen as golden chains of future revenue not just a one-off, hit and run sale. Customers are just too expensive to attract and too valuable to loose after one or two transactions.

Even if your customer buying cycle is infrequent, for example a major car purchase, the customer can still benefit from support, and opportunities for extra sales can be identified.

The three principles of customer-focused selling

The following key principles are drawn from customer-focused organisations. Typically, these organisations are able to develop a high-level of customer satisfaction (from how they are sold to) and demonstrate a higher level of retention, repeat business and referral (all things I recommend you measure as part of your sales analysis).

The customer-focused salesperson applies three principles at every step of the sales process. These are:

1. Focus on the customer
2. Establish credibility
3. Persuade through involvement.

Principle	Actions
Focus on the customer	▶ View the customer as the centre of the sales process. Concentrate on the customer's buying steps, rather than on your sales process or agenda. ▶ Make everything you say or do vital to the sales interaction and of value to the customer.
Establish credibility	▶ Ask questions after the customer understands why sharing information is important. ▶ Propose a situation after the customer perceives his or her need as urgent. ▶ Close after the customer has sufficient information to make a decision.
Persuade through involvement	▶ Allow the customer to give information. ▶ Talk less and listen more. ▶ View opposition as a sign of involvement. ▶ Help the customer to solve the problem or meet a need.

Figure 5: The customer-focused sales process

Put simply, it is important to give the customer a very positive experience of buying, not being sold to. It is generally held that most customers dislike the 'pushy' sales approach. Therefore, these principles help to promote a more 'pulley' skill set.

Customer-focused selling skills

There are six customer-focused selling skills, each with a separate function. These skills are a basic requirement for effective customer-focused selling:

1. Connecting
2. Encouraging
3. Questioning
4. Listening
5. Confirming
6. Providing.

These skills are equally relevant whether you are working to meet the needs of a customer and his or her organisation or working with an associate to meet mutual, personal, and organisational needs.

The customer's buying steps

During the sales process, the customer goes through a series of buying steps. Each step reflects how the customer feels at various stages of the relationship during the sales process. It is important that the customer-focused salesperson is more sensitive that normal – timing is more important than technique in this context. Generalised sales resistance will be generated unnecessarily if the sales approach becomes out of sequence with the customers' buying cycle or interest level.

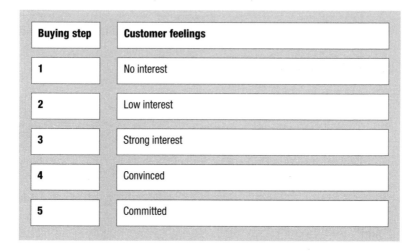

Buying step	Customer feelings
1	No interest
2	Low interest
3	Strong interest
4	Convinced
5	Committed

Figure 6: The customers' buying steps

At each step, there is a sales strategy that enables the salesperson to help the customer progress up the buying steps.

No interest

In many situations, your prospect (customer) may have little or no interest in your product or service initially. At this point you are in the 'prospecting' phase of the sales process. It is important to contact the customer proactively to generate more interest. The approach should be personalised as much as possible and based on what is known about the customer or customer group. Typically, it should be something new, or a specific interest or something that is different in some way.

Low interest

At the second step, your customer may have a low interest in your project or services. To move to the next buying step, you must explore and get significant information about:

▶ The customer

▶ His or her situation

▶ The needs and the problems the customer is trying to address.

Spend more time and attention on this step of the process than any other. There are two areas you need to address:

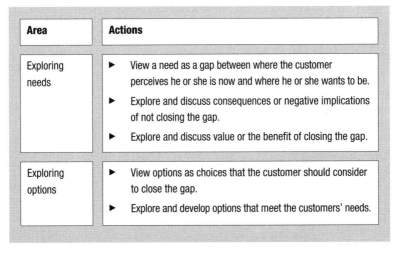

Area	Actions
Exploring needs	▶ View a need as a gap between where the customer perceives he or she is now and where he or she wants to be. ▶ Explore and discuss consequences or negative implications of not closing the gap. ▶ Explore and discuss value or the benefit of closing the gap.
Exploring options	▶ View options as choices that the customer should consider to close the gap. ▶ Explore and develop options that meet the customers' needs.

Figure 7: The customers' needs and options

By using the data gathered about the customer's transaction and buying interests, the timing and content of these first two stages can be accurately defined. For example, a mail-order office supplies company can time and personalise mailings to arrive just before an order might be placed, based on previous order patterns, and products can be promoted that are both regularly ordered or identified as 'gaps' – that is they are not ordered but could or should be.

Strong interest

At the third step your customer has strong interest in your product or service. Now you must propose solutions. To propose solutions and make an effective presentation, link customer needs to the benefits that your customer can derive from your product or service.

As most markets are ferociously competitive, often price or 'special offer' concessions or incentives are used to encourage first time customers to try a product or service. Hence the importance of converting that one time customer into a long-term 'client' or advocate. If possible, differentiate on service and superior purchasing convenience or experience.

Convinced

At the fourth step, your customer is convinced that your product or service will meet his' or hers' needs. To move to the final step, you must close the sale. It is the logical outcome of an effective presentation. The close should be:

▶ Direct

▶ Concise

▶ Non-manipulative.

Committed

An effective close takes the customer to the fifth and final step, in which the customer is committed to your product or service as the means of meeting his or her need.

By focusing on your customer's buying steps, you are seeing the situation from the customer's point of view. It is critical that you stay in touch with the customer's progress throughout the buying process.

The biggest impediment to successful sales calls is the inclination to close at the wrong time. If your customer is at the low interest phase, it is not appropriate to be presenting solutions or closing. You have not earned the right. Be perceptive and remain flexible.

It may not be necessary to move the customer through all of the buying steps. You may encounter a customer anywhere in the buying process.

Depending on the customers' specific needs, you will need to shape your approach to the sales process.

You must perceive where the customer is in the buying process and devise your sales strategy accordingly.

Customer-focused prospecting

How to define your ideal customer

Before you begin to pick up the phone, or write a letter, the starting point is to target the ideal customers, or ideal potential customers.

One of the best places to start in finding your ideal customer is with your existing customers. List down 10-30 of your current active and successful customers. Think about what kind of company, organisation or individuals that they are.

If you sell to businesses consider the size, nature and location of the company. Whereabouts are they based geographically? What kind of business are they in? What are their size, turnover and other factors that may influence their suitability?

What sort of attitude must they have towards your products or services? What facts would you need to check for to make them a suitable prospect? Who would it be best to contact within that organisation? Is there anybody else that you could also contact who may be easier to get through to on an initial call?

If you sell to individuals or consumers, you may want to consider what time of day is best to catch your potential prospects in, what are their ages, hobbies, background, social status, income etc?

The importance of carefully targeting ideal customers is twofold. The first is that we make greater use of our time; by not wasting time with people or companies who can't or won't buy, we can increase our chances that our time spent prospecting will pay off.

We can also protect ourselves from some of the rejection that may come with telephoning for appointments. It is no secret that when you are prospecting by telephone, you are going to get a lot more 'no's' than you might do when you are seeing people face-to-face.

Referrals

One of the most effective and ultimately most successful ways of gaining new business, is by referrals. If you have not done so I would recommend that you take time to contact as many existing customers and prospects as possible and gain two or three possible referrals from each.

Put these at the top of your list for calling for an appointment. However, take time to establish from the customer that refers you the lead, whether or not they are happy for you to use their company name when contacting that referral. Their wishes and confidentiality must be maintained at all times, if you are going to be able to go back to them again for further referrals.

Organised persistence

Organised persistence is the name given to the end result of keeping an accurate call back system with accurate record keeping. It will enable you to select the very best prospects and customers, and keep with them and move with them as they develop their sales needs and requirements. Remember some customers will buy very quickly and others may take much longer. Your job as a sales professional is to sell professionally in a way which is in sympathy with how customers want to buy. By all means we need to influence people and help them make quicker decisions, but at all times it must be respectful to their buying criteria and procedure.

Staying in touch

One of the things that many top sales professionals have found, particularly those selling ongoing products and services to businesses, is that it is good to stay in touch with existing customers and prospects. When a customer buys once it is usually only a trial purchase. You need to keep in contact with those customers with something new, interesting or different on a regular basis. When you are selling to businesses 90 days is a normal business quarter and is seen as being neither too pushy, nor too infrequent to miss opportunities.

Don't forget today's customers

However, before you do any cold calling, warm calling or anything else, make sure you stay in regular contact – about once every three months for example – with all the customer's that you have today. The tragedy is that every year sales people, and businesses, lose 10, 20, 30, 50 per cent and more of their existing customers – and often they don't even know who those customers or contacts are.

Take time to collect the following information every month, and act on it:

▶ List all your top customers – the top 20 per cent by number and calculate the percentage sales contribution they make individually and as a group.

▶ List all customers that have not purchased in the last X months – whatever is appropriate in your business. My suggestion would be that every customer should get a call once every three months, just as courtesy.

▶ List all the customers who have spent more this year/month than last; contact them and find out why, and say 'thank you', and also tell them about something new, interesting or different.

▶ List all the customers, who have spent less this period than last, contact them and find out why, and tell them about something new, interesting or different.

- ▶ Plan renewal, replacement, upgrade or diversification. Make sure your product development and marketing work together to give existing customers a compelling reason to keep buying from you, or stay in touch in-between purchasers.

- ▶ Drive the relationship down to every level within a customer's organisation.

- ▶ Remember that you have more to fear from complacency than competitors.

Building a business pipeline

1. Every week, select ten companies or organisations that meet your 'target' market profile. List these names, addresses and phone numbers. Select these carefully and include referrals.

2. Make a research call to each and identify the most appropriate initial contact. You do not need to speak to this person at this stage, talk to the receptionist or assistant instead.

3. Send a one page 'success' letter and a very brief (one side of A4) overview of what (benefits) you can offer. Mail on a Thursday or Friday. Focus on your capabilities and how you can benefit the prospect.

4. Telephone each 'suspect' that you mailed within 3-5 days. As 50 per cent will be unavailable, log callbacks in your diary. Don't be surprised if they don't remember your letter, review it on the phone. Dropping names or using benefits by association can be useful.

5. Have a prepared call sheet, questions and reasons for an appointment (your goal is a short initial meeting). Offer a benefit to your meeting: share ideas, examples, etc.

6. Set aside time each week for research, mailing and planning – consistency is vital for this to work. You might find it better to aim for one hour a day rather than one whole day each week.

7. Maintain accurate but brief reports to monitor your progress and to track activity.

8. After approximately 10-12 weeks of contacting new suspects, reduce the new contacts by between 50 per cent and 80 per cent and instead go back through all those people you contacted previously and re-contact them, i.e. stay in touch with suspects and prospects every three months. Things often change and if you have selected potential prospects well, it may only be a matter of time before you do business.

9. Make sure that the subsequent 90 day contact contains something new, interesting or different, even if only very slightly. This also makes sure that you don't appear too pushy.

10. No matter how busy you get, always make time to keep in touch with new suspects and prospects in this way on a planned and consistent basis.

The 'three rules':

1. Do not allow any one customer to contribute more than 30 per cent of you sales in any given quarter.

2. Make sure that at least 30 per cent of your sales pipeline is from new business, the rest should be from existing customers or referrals. (Be careful not to rely on existing customers to the exclusion of new customers.)

3. Always have a third more sales in the pipeline than you need.

Capability statements

The sales strategy that you should use to proceed to the second phase is the capability statement. A capability statement describes the benefits of working with a sales person and relates them to the probable needs of that particular customer or group of customers.

Making a good first impression on first time sales calls

Any sales interaction or discussion with a customer has three essential components:

1. **Opening** – To ensure a mutually agreeable purpose.

2. **Progressing** – To move towards accomplishing the purpose.

3. **Concluding** – To clarify the progress of the discussion and to set up the next action step.

Opening the call

It is important to see any prospect as a potential long-term customer. Patience and preparation now will pay long-term dividends later. The opening consists of three steps:

1. **Purpose** – State why you are contacting the customer.

2. **Benefit** – Explain the benefit of spending time with you to the customer.

3. **Check** – Ask if the customer agrees with your agenda.

Benefits of preparing

Prepare your opening before you make the call – whether it is a face-to-face call or a telephone call. A good opening will:

▶ Align expectations between you and the customer

▶ Show that you are organised

▶ Show concern for making the best use of the customer's time

▶ Open up communication with the customer.

Establishing a purpose agreeable to the customer early in the conversation is a key differentiator between successful and unsuccessful discussions.

Capability statements – initial customer contact

A capability statement describes the overall benefits of working with a customer and relates them to their needs. For example: 'We have a variety of publications that can attract new customers to you and encourage existing customers to spend more.'

Preparing

The capability statement should be prepared before your first sales call. A prepared capability statement should answer two questions before they are asked:

▶ Why?

▶ Why you (the salesperson)?

Guidelines

The capability statement should:

▶ Set the stage for a common understanding

▶ Link capabilities to probable needs

▶ Be based on as much knowledge as you can obtain about both the prospect's industry and particular situation

▶ Be brief; not a product or service presentation

▶ Not overload the customer with benefits, since you do not yet know much detail about the customer's needs

▶ Be specific enough to be interesting

▶ Be broad enough not to close off options.

Note: Avoid pitching specifics (features and benefits) of the product at this point.

Progressing the call

When progressing a sales call you should demonstrate to the customer that you may be able to help him or her solve important problems. The capability statement should:

1. Be tailored to the specific industry

2. Include the pertinent benefits your company can offer that industry.

Note: These benefits, however, are not the same as the benefits presented in the opening statement, which shows the customer the advantage of investing time in this particular call. The capability statement should be delivered after the customer has agreed to the purpose of the call.

Examples

1. Open the call

▶   Stating the purpose – to explore ways in which you might help the customer's company meet its goals.

▶   Stating the benefit – investing time in the call might provide some new information about products and services that the customer could find useful.

▶   Checking – to gain agreement to the purpose.

2. Progress the call

▶   Qualifying the prospect.

▶   Delivering a capability statement, if needed, by describing the ways in which your company has helped companies, such as the customer's, solve similar problems.

Keeping it simple

Keep your conversation with the prospect on a more general and conceptual level. Do not get drawn into nitty-gritty details, or you may find yourself in deeper then you want. If you find a customer who wants to hear your pitch, try to 'defuse and defer'. Remember that your purpose in making the initial call is to get an appointment, not to tell the prospect everything that you have to offer.

Customer-focused selling skills

As mentioned briefly at the beginning of the chapter, customer-focused selling skills can be used to progress a discussion. However, the sequence in which you use those skills, and the emphasis you give them, will vary.

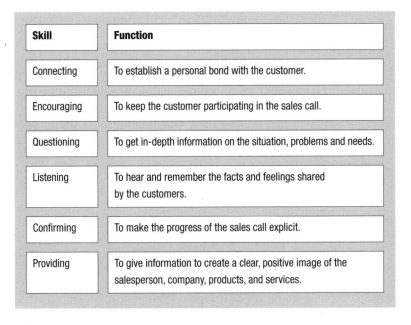

Skill	Function
Connecting	To establish a personal bond with the customer.
Encouraging	To keep the customer participating in the sales call.
Questioning	To get in-depth information on the situation, problems and needs.
Listening	To hear and remember the facts and feelings shared by the customers.
Confirming	To make the progress of the sales call explicit.
Providing	To give information to create a clear, positive image of the salesperson, company, products, and services.

Figure 8: Customer-focused selling skills

Connecting

Connecting skills are used to establish a personal bond, resulting in rapport between you and the customer.

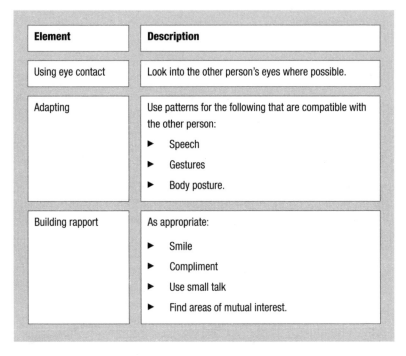

Element	Description
Using eye contact	Look into the other person's eyes where possible.
Adapting	Use patterns for the following that are compatible with the other person: ► Speech ► Gestures ► Body posture.
Building rapport	As appropriate: ► Smile ► Compliment ► Use small talk ► Find areas of mutual interest.

Figure 9: Connecting skills

Encouraging

Encouraging skills are used to keep the other person participating in the discussion, resulting in interaction.

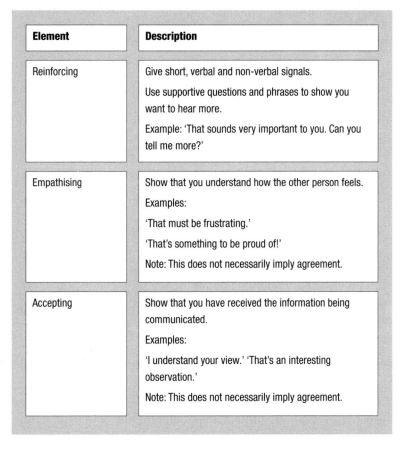

Element	Description
Reinforcing	Give short, verbal and non-verbal signals. Use supportive questions and phrases to show you want to hear more. Example: 'That sounds very important to you. Can you tell me more?'
Empathising	Show that you understand how the other person feels. Examples: 'That must be frustrating.' 'That's something to be proud of!' Note: This does not necessarily imply agreement.
Accepting	Show that you have received the information being communicated. Examples: 'I understand your view.' 'That's an interesting observation.' Note: This does not necessarily imply agreement.

Figure 10: Encouraging skills

Questioning

Questioning skills are used to obtain in-depth information about the situation, problems and needs of the other person, resulting in information obtained from the customer.

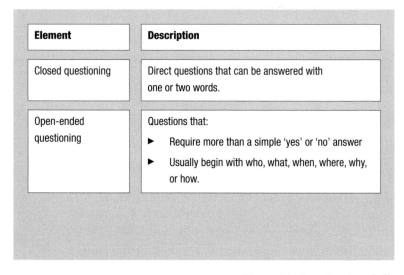

Element	Description
Closed questioning	Direct questions that can be answered with one or two words.
Open-ended questioning	Questions that: ► Require more than a simple 'yes' or 'no' answer ► Usually begin with who, what, when, where, why, or how.

Figure 11: Questioning skills

Listening

Listening skills are used to discover what your customer needs and expects from you and your company. While listening is a separate skill, it is also a critical umbrella skill for all of the customer-focused selling skills, resulting in your understanding of customer needs and feelings.

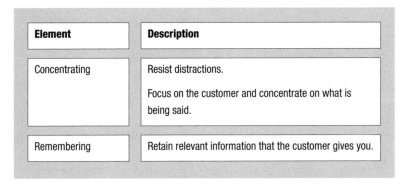

Element	Description
Concentrating	Resist distractions. Focus on the customer and concentrate on what is being said.
Remembering	Retain relevant information that the customer gives you.

Figure 12: Listening skills

Types of listening

Questioning and listening are vital and must be at a higher level than in conventional telephone or face-to-face selling.

Listening ranges from being attentive to being active:

▶ Attentive listening is comprehending and remembering

▶ Reflective listening retains information, evaluates, and draws inferences

▶ Active listening gives verbal or non-verbal feedback to the speaker.

Confirming

Confirming skills make the progress of the discussion explicit, resulting in agreement.

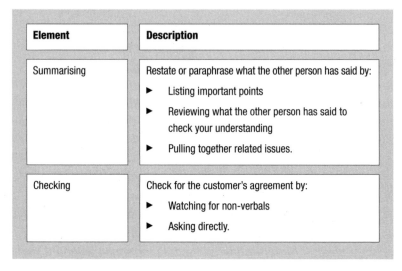

Element	Description
Summarising	Restate or paraphrase what the other person has said by: ▶ Listing important points ▶ Reviewing what the other person has said to check your understanding ▶ Pulling together related issues.
Checking	Check for the customer's agreement by: ▶ Watching for non-verbals ▶ Asking directly.

Figure 13: Confirming skills

Providing

Providing skills are used to give information to the other person that:

► Are responsive to the needs of the situation

► Create a positive image of you and your ability to address those needs

► Result in customer satisfaction.

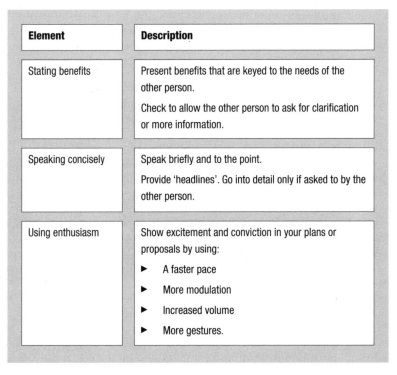

Element	Description
Stating benefits	Present benefits that are keyed to the needs of the other person. Check to allow the other person to ask for clarification or more information.
Speaking concisely	Speak briefly and to the point. Provide 'headlines'. Go into detail only if asked to by the other person.
Using enthusiasm	Show excitement and conviction in your plans or proposals by using: ► A faster pace ► More modulation ► Increased volume ► More gestures.

Figure 14: Providing skills

Handling objections, queries and concerns

Objections can arise in any sales situation, and at any point in the process. At the beginning, when you are phone prospecting, you may encounter resistance from 'gatekeepers' or from your intended contact person. At the end, when you are trying to close the sale, objections are typical.

In order to encourage long-term customer satisfaction and loyalty, dialogue about objections, queries and concerns must be conducted early and often. In essence, welcome complaints and concerns – seek them and anticipate them.

The potential benefits of handling objections well

Objections must be resolved, or the customer may be lost. Many sales-people are uncomfortable about handling objections and feel threatened by them. However, objections should be viewed as poten-tially beneficial because they:

▶ Are a natural part of the buying process. Getting answers to ques-tions and resolving doubts is a normal behaviour pattern in buying

▶ Present an opportunity for educating the customer, as well as for getting more information from the customer

▶ Reveal the customer's concerns and give you a chance to encourage the customer to became more involved in the sales call

▶ Can result in enhanced trust and a better relationship, if handled well

▶ Show that the customer is actively interested, and not keeping objections a secret.

The objection handling process

The process for handling objections uses customer-focused selling skills in the following sequence:

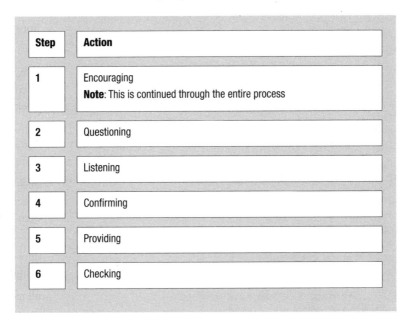

Step	Action
1	Encouraging **Note**: This is continued through the entire process
2	Questioning
3	Listening
4	Confirming
5	Providing
6	Checking

Figure 15: Handling objections

This process applies to how you should deal with objections wherever they occur in the sales process.

Step 1: Encouraging

Statements such as 'I can see how you would be concerned about that', 'I hear you', or 'Can you tell me more about that?' are examples of encouraging the customer.

Encouraging is the most important and difficult step because it runs counter to what most people do when they feel they are being 'attacked'.

Key encouraging actions

▶ Do not try to answer the objection at this point.

▶ Acknowledge the customer's right to object and indicate your willingness to let the customer express his or her reservations completely.

▶ Listen carefully to what he or she has to say.

▶ Show empathy. Understand how the customer feels by putting yourself in his or her place.

▶ Use this step to begin thinking about the best way to resolve the objection.

▶ Encouraging the customer is not the same as agreeing with the customer. You do not need to agree with the customer's opinion. You do need to agree with his or hers right to express honest feelings during the sales call.

▶ When in doubt, ask the customer to elaborate.

Step 2: Questioning

Frequently, the real objection is different from what the customer first expressed. Ask questions to:

▶ Clarify the objection

▶ Discover the customer's specific concern.

For example, 'What is the nature of your concern?' 'What are your biggest reservations?'

Key questioning actions

▶ Do not assume that you understand the objection.

▶ Do not belittle the questioning phase or appear to cross-examine the customer.

▶ Encourage the customer to keep him or her involved.

Step 3: Listening

When the customer talks, listen attentively for:

▶ Feelings the person seems to be conveying

▶ Factual information that he or she is sharing with you.

Key listening actions

Take notes to remind you of key points to return to at a later date.

▶ Do not interrupt

▶ Actively listen, so you really understand the objection.

Step 4: Confirming

Check your understanding of the problem before responding. Before you proceed, you must:

▶ Know what the customer is thinking

▶ Demonstrate that you understand the objection.

Key confirming actions

▶ Summarise what you have heard.

▶ Check your understanding with the customer.

Step 5: Providing

You should answer the objection as specifically as possible. Objections and their appropriate responses usually fall into one of four general categories:

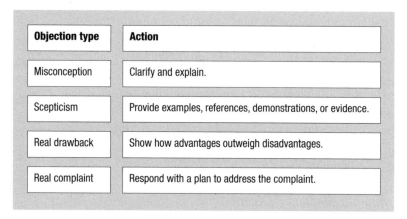

Objection type	Action
Misconception	Clarify and explain.
Scepticism	Provide examples, references, demonstrations, or evidence.
Real drawback	Show how advantages outweigh disadvantages.
Real complaint	Respond with a plan to address the complaint.

Figure 16: Objection types

Step 6: Checking

Check to see if the customer's objection has been resolved. You might ask outright if your response has been satisfactory. If not, start the process again by encouraging the customer and by asking questions to draw out the real objection.

Key checking actions

▶   Ask the customer directly if they are satisfied with the resolution.

▶   If not, repeat the six-step process.

Exploring needs

A need is a gap

Exploring needs is a process of uncovering the gaps between a customer's perception of his or her present state of affairs and his or her desired state of affairs. In other words:

▶ Where is the customer's organisation now?

▶ Where does he or she want it to be?

This can be envisioned as a physical gap. A need is defined as the gap between the customer's present state and desired state.

Categories

Customers have a wide range of needs, but any of them can be classified into two broad categories. These are needs related to:

▶ Increasing something

▶ Decreasing something.

Defining the gap

Not every customer has explicitly defined the gap between his or her present state and desired state. Defining the gap requires converting vaguely defined problems into clear statements of need. The more concrete and explicit the statement, the more likely the customer is to recognise the need to take action.

Prepare for a customer call by speculating about the customer's probable needs. You can often identify the general needs your potential customers may have before beginning formal discussions with them. This general understanding of problems can then be a springboard for a more detailed exploration of needs.

Needs of discussion will vary depending on your style, the customer, and the situation. Here are some guidelines:

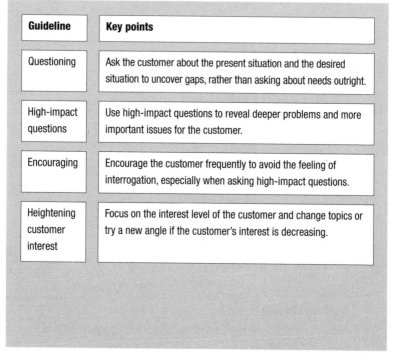

Guideline	Key points
Questioning	Ask the customer about the present situation and the desired situation to uncover gaps, rather than asking about needs outright.
High-impact questions	Use high-impact questions to reveal deeper problems and more important issues for the customer.
Encouraging	Encourage the customer frequently to avoid the feeling of interrogation, especially when asking high-impact questions.
Heightening customer interest	Focus on the interest level of the customer and change topics or try a new angle if the customer's interest is decreasing.

Figure 17: Defining the gap

High-impact questions

High-impact questions maximise the sales call by returning high-value information in an efficient amount of time.

High-impact questions = high value information

High-impact questions require customers to think, organise information, and search for new meanings to existing information before responding. They ask customers to:

► Evaluate or analyse

► Speculate

► Express feelings

► React.

The result is the type of information you might hear if you were to attend a customer's problem solving or planning session. Good high-impact questions make customers say:

'Gee...I don't know. I never thought about that.'

'Hmm...I never put those ideas together that way before.'

Criteria

High-impact questions should be:

► Brief and clear

► Open-ended

► Phrased to require a thoughtful answer

► Relevant to the customer's situation and position.

Benefits

Using high-impact questions in sales calls has several benefits to you. High-impact questions are likely to:

► Involve the customer by requiring him or her to think

► Increase the amount of time that customers talk

► Provide new insights into problems

► Produce high-quality information

► Expose underlying issues

► Result in salespeople being seen as perceptive professionals who can function as consultants

► Cause the customer to believe that the sales call was valuable.

Comparison to open-ended questions

Open-ended questions invite customers to respond with more than a 'yes' or 'no' answer. However, open-ended questions may elicit factual information that could easily be found in files, annual reports, or organisational charts.

Customers who enjoy talking about their organisations or themselves may respond willingly to open-ended questions for a while, since it allows them to talk. However, such conversations do not usually require customers to engage in high-level thinking, nor are they likely to produce any new insights of value for them.

Tips for high-impact questions

▶ Prepare high-impact questions to use with a customer as part of your sales tool kit.

▶ Once in front of a customer, you may use these prepared questions or devise others spontaneously in response to points the customer has raised.

Encourage the customer

High-impact questions are tough to answer. If you do not encourage while questioning, the customer may feel interrogated. By encouraging frequently, you can take the edge off your high-impact questions and make the section more conversational.

Listening

While listening is a separate customer-focused selling skill, it is also an umbrella over all other skills. Effective listening is critical to building customer-focused relationships.

Listening for needs

Customers express needs in different ways. Not all needs will be overtly expressed. You should listen for the following three types of needs.

Need	Description	Example
Stated	Clear statement by customer of what is needed.	I need to attract new customers.
Implied	Need is expressed in a vague way.	My boss is concerned about the number of customers that walk past our stores.
Hidden	Recognised by you, but not by the customer.	We do everything we can think of to make our exterior appealing in an effort to attract passing foot traffic into the stores.

Figure 18: Listening for needs

Four types of listening behaviour to avoid

There are four main unproductive listening behaviours that should be avoided:

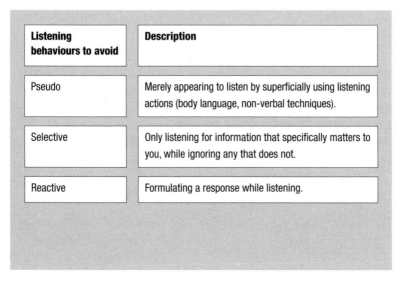

Listening behaviours to avoid	Description
Pseudo	Merely appearing to listen by superficially using listening actions (body language, non-verbal techniques).
Selective	Only listening for information that specifically matters to you, while ignoring any that does not.
Reactive	Formulating a response while listening.

Figure 19: Listening behaviours to avoid

Tips for customer-focused listening

▶ Listen for pivotal words, ideas, concepts and needs, and incorporate them into your response.

▶ Interpret importance, priority, and implications.

▶ Observe and use appropriate body language.

▶ Take notes to focus on customer needs.

Understanding the buying criteria and the customer's buying process

Needs are not enough

In developing long-term customer opportunities, needs, consequences and pay-offs are essential, but not quite enough in themselves. It is also necessary to understand something of the customer's buying criteria and process. Whilst you might choose to develop a set of headings to suit your own business and customers, the following are adequate for most sales situations:

▶ Money, budget, cost expectation

▶ Authority levels and buying influences

▶ Timescales – both to implement and place an order

▶ Competition and alternatives

▶ Hot buttons – how the decision will be made.

Each of these will combine to create a unique buying or customer 'fingerprint' for each sales opportunity or transaction. Here are some examples of questions that might be used to define these accurately:

Money, budget, cost expectation

▶ What is your budget for this item/project?

▶ How much are you expecting to spend?

▶ What is the range of prices that you have been quoted?

▶ How is your spending in this area split between different suppliers?

▶ How flexible is your budget?

▶ What payment or finance methods are you considering?

Authority levels and buying influences

▶ Apart from yourself, who else is involved in this decision?

▶ Who else will be involved, and in what way?

▶ What is your next step from here?

► How will the decision be made and reviewed?

► Who is assessing the technical and financial aspects?

Timescales – both to implement and place an order

► When is the earliest you would like to start using the system?

► When is the latest you need delivery by?

► When do you expect to make a decision?

► How long will it take to agree this?

► What are your timescales?

Competition and alternatives

► What other alternatives are you considering?

► What other models and quotes are you looking at?

► What are you not considering?

Hot-buttons – how the decision will be made

► What is most important to you in choosing the right solution?

► Apart from price, what are your most important considerations?

► How will you know when you have found what you are looking for?

► How did you choose and make a decision on the last X that you purchased?

► What information can I provide that will help you make a decision?

► What is it that you do not want?

Exploring and developing options

Linkage to driving principles

Exploring and developing options is linked to the driving principles.

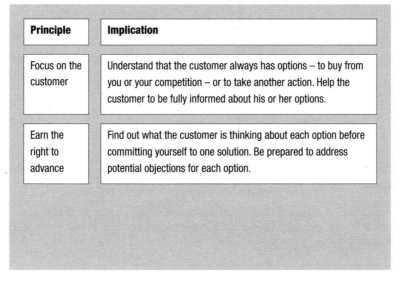

Principle	Implication
Focus on the customer	Understand that the customer always has options – to buy from you or your competition – or to take another action. Help the customer to be fully informed about his or her options.
Earn the right to advance	Find out what the customer is thinking about each option before committing yourself to one solution. Be prepared to address potential objections for each option.

Figure 20: The driving principles

Once you have determined a need and outlined the consequences and value associated with it, your next action step is to develop a solution. At this point in the buying process, a customer considers options to solve the problem. It is important that you can be involved in helping the customer analyse the options and determine which one is best.

Persuade through involvement

Customers would rather buy a product than be sold a product: helping and working with customers to explore options allows them to be involved in selecting a solution that meets their needs – it allows them to buy.

The more involved customers are in selecting options, the more willing they are to buy. Remember: the best way to persuade is through involvement.

By participating in a customer's analysis of which option to select, you increase the chances that the final choice will be one of your solutions. Through this process, you draw the customer into the sale and allow him or her to sell him or herself on the solution that best meets his or hers needs.

Exploring options may be completed in three simple steps:

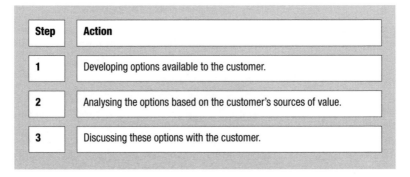

Step	Action
1	Developing options available to the customer.
2	Analysing the options based on the customer's sources of value.
3	Discussing these options with the customer.

Figure 21: The three steps in exploring options

Step 1: Developing options

Developing options requires you to look at all of the options available to the customer. They can choose to:

▶ Buy, or keep buying from you

▶ Buy, or keep buying from your competition

▶ Take another action (for example, do nothing).

Earn the right

Developing all options and putting these options on the table helps earn you the right to participate in the analysis of all options. This may allow you the opportunity to differentiate your solutions from those of the competition by enhancing the basic solution with variations, such as:

▶ Customer service and support arrangements

▶ Implementation arrangements

▶ Submission and payment arrangements.

Step 2: Analysing options

Exploring the range of options is an important, but often neglected, step in the sales process. Salespeople who skip this step convince themselves that once they know the customer's needs, they also know the best solution; however, by not exploring options, they:

▶ Deny the customer the right to participate in discovering that solution

▶ Lose sales because their proposed solution does not seem right to the customer.

Using an option matrix

There are many ways to analyse options. One way is to use a tool called an option matrix, to help you organise the options that you are considering.

There are two versions of the option matrix:

▶ One with the 'potential objections' column

▶ One without the 'potential objections' column.

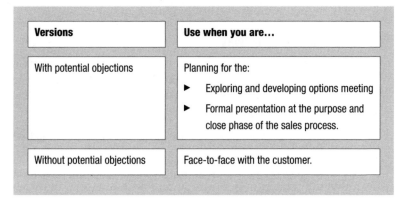

Versions	Use when you are...
With potential objections	Planning for the: ▶ Exploring and developing options meeting ▶ Formal presentation at the purpose and close phase of the sales process.
Without potential objections	Face-to-face with the customer.

Figure 22: Versions of the option matrix

When to use the option matrix

There are three uses for the option matrix tool:

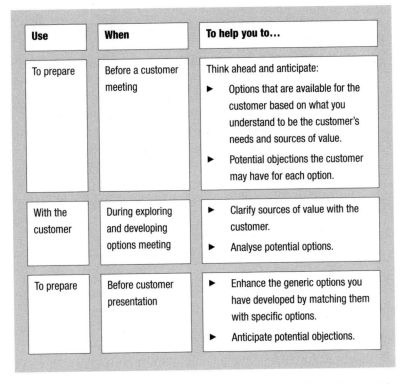

Use	When	To help you to...
To prepare	Before a customer meeting	Think ahead and anticipate: ▶ Options that are available for the customer based on what you understand to be the customer's needs and sources of value. ▶ Potential objections the customer may have for each option.
With the customer	During exploring and developing options meeting	▶ Clarify sources of value with the customer. ▶ Analyse potential options.
To prepare	Before customer presentation	▶ Enhance the generic options you have developed by matching them with specific options. ▶ Anticipate potential objections.

Figure 23: When to use the option matrix

How to use the option matrix

Follow these steps to use the option matrix:

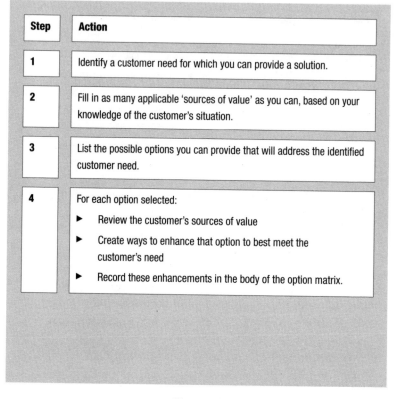

Step	Action
1	Identify a customer need for which you can provide a solution.
2	Fill in as many applicable 'sources of value' as you can, based on your knowledge of the customer's situation.
3	List the possible options you can provide that will address the identified customer need.
4	For each option selected: ▶ Review the customer's sources of value ▶ Create ways to enhance that option to best meet the customer's need ▶ Record these enhancements in the body of the option matrix.

Figure 24: How to use the option matrix

Step 3: Discussing options

Process

Once you have generated options, discuss them with the customer, using the following process.

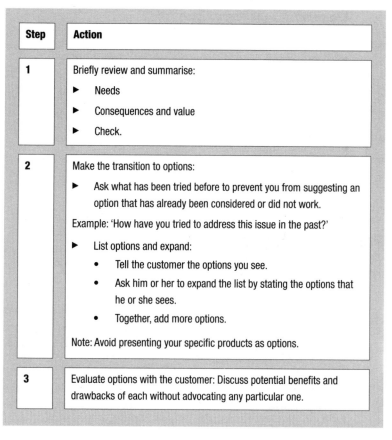

Step	Action
1	Briefly review and summarise: ▶ Needs ▶ Consequences and value ▶ Check.
2	Make the transition to options: ▶ Ask what has been tried before to prevent you from suggesting an option that has already been considered or did not work. Example: 'How have you tried to address this issue in the past?' ▶ List options and expand: • Tell the customer the options you see. • Ask him or her to expand the list by stating the options that he or she sees. • Together, add more options. Note: Avoid presenting your specific products as options.
3	Evaluate options with the customer: Discuss potential benefits and drawbacks of each without advocating any particular one.

Figure 25: Discussing options

Key points of discussing options

▶ Do not advocate your product or service too early.

▶ Draw out the customer's perception of which option is best.

▶ Do not confuse the customer with too many choices.

▶ Be prepared to handle potential customer objections raised for each option.

Key points of exploring options

You must remember to:

▶ Understand the need

▶ Understand the customer's sources of value

▶ Select product/service options

▶ Enhance the options

▶ Do your homework/be creative

▶ Involve the customer.

Proposing and closing

When proposing solutions the salesperson moves from exploration to advocacy.

However, making a proposal entails much more than just trying to convince the customer to buy the product. The idea of using a 'canned sales pitch' with multiple customers is obsolete in today's sophisticated, needs-oriented market.

Proposing does not necessarily mean a formal presentation in front of a large group of people with slides and a projector. Proposing can be done one-on-one and informally – across the desk from your customer or in a meeting with a few key decision-makers.

Linkage to the driving principles

The driving principles are pivotal in the strategy for proposing solutions.

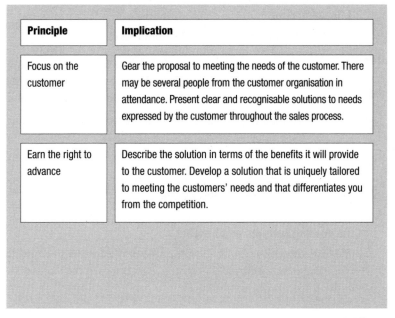

Principle	Implication
Focus on the customer	Gear the proposal to meeting the needs of the customer. There may be several people from the customer organisation in attendance. Present clear and recognisable solutions to needs expressed by the customer throughout the sales process.
Earn the right to advance	Describe the solution in terms of the benefits it will provide to the customer. Develop a solution that is uniquely tailored to meeting the customers' needs and that differentiates you from the competition.

Figure 26: The driving principles

Proposing solutions: overview

Whether your proposal is formal or informal, it should be:

▶ Well organised

▶ Well prepared

▶ Customer-focused.

Some general guidelines for proposals are:

▶ Tailor them to the needs of the customer

▶ Be concise and to the point

▶ Show the customer that he or she is important to you

▶ Differentiate yourself from your competitors.

Features and benefits

Knowing the difference between a feature and a benefit will help you to obtain a favourable response from a customer, increasing the possibility of making a sale.

► A feature is a characteristic of a product or service.

However, people do not buy a product for its features. They buy a product because its features can help them accomplish something – in other words, because those features provide certain benefits.

► A benefit is a way in which one or more features of the product provide a definable advantage, improvement, or satisfaction for the buyer.

Features are what a product is or does, whereas benefits are what the product provides for the customer.

Discussing features and benefits

When conducting a discussion with a customer on features and benefits, you need to be aware of what each person brings to the discussion.

What the customer brings	What the salesperson brings
A set of general problems that may be translated into specific statements of needs.	A range of products and services that have many features capable of providing an array of potential benefits to customers.

Needs can be personal as well as organisational. A statement such as 'we need to increase store traffic' expresses an organisational need. But your customer might also indicate a need to look good to his or her boss – a personal need.

The salesperson brings only potential benefits until the benefits can be shown to meet specific customer needs.

Focus on the customer's needs to have the right perspective for discussing benefits. The purpose of discussing features and benefits is to:

► Convert general problems to specific needs

► Link those needs to the benefits of your products or services

► Explain those benefits and features.

In this way, you bring the customer's problem together with your specific product or service.

Focus on providing the customer with clearly recognisable benefits that address his or her expressed needs. Remember that the customer defines value or benefit.

Guidelines

Some guidelines for discussing features and benefits are:

► Recap the need, then go to the benefit

► State the benefit first, than cite the appropriate feature

► Translate features into desired benefits.

Use a transitional phrase such as 'that's because', to tie the benefits that address specific needs to the feature. The method immediately answers the question 'What's in it for me?' for the customer.

If you state the product feature first, connect it with the phrase 'this means for you', followed by a statement of the benefit.

Proposing solutions

At this point, you should explain how the benefits of your solution could meet the customer's needs. It should not be assumed that the customer will take your words as proof and instantly believe them. You can make your proposal convincing by using the 5E's:

5E's	Key point
1 Examples Make it real	Illustrate a customer situation similar to your current customer's to make a stronger case for your solution. Example: 'For example, by accepting the card, the ABC Establishment, similar to yours, increased annual sales by 10 per cent last year.'
2 Enthusiasm Give it feeling	Ideas conveyed with feeling are more persuasive than dry statements of fact. Be enthusiastic – often final decisions are made based on how the customer feels after hearing you.
3 Evidence Make it clear	Provide data to prove an idea's effectiveness. Data should be verified and valid or the audience may note its inapplicability or inaccuracies, challenge your sources, and become alienated. Avoid 'data dumping'.
4 Experts Make it credible	Use references from experts to show that you are speaking with objectivity, not from personal bias. Let the audience know who the expert is and, if the person is not known universally, preface the name with a title or description.

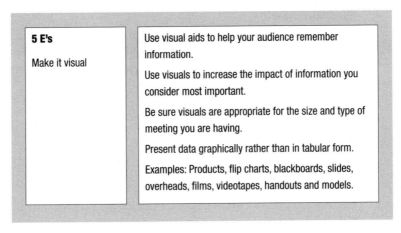

5 E's	Use visual aids to help your audience remember information.
Make it visual	Use visuals to increase the impact of information you consider most important.
	Be sure visuals are appropriate for the size and type of meeting you are having.
	Present data graphically rather than in tabular form.
	Examples: Products, flip charts, blackboards, slides, overheads, films, videotapes, handouts and models.

Figure 27: The 5E's model

Exploring value

This is the perfect point at which to elicit customer involvement. Presumably, you have already presented the solutions in terms of benefits that best meet the customer's needs. Now you must expand on the benefits by exploring the value of implementing the solutions you have provided.

Objections

Throughout the proposal, be prepared to handle objections:

▶ Think of objections as neutral or positive signs that mean the customer is paying attention and is considering your ideas

▶ Anticipate objections early and have answers to questions that may be posed

▶ Listen carefully to the objections and take your time responding to them, using the model for handling objections.

Handling delays

In the sales process, especially in the final phases, delays can represent a frustrating grey area that leaves you hanging, wondering whether or not the customer will buy. After you have proposed a solution, one of three outcomes could take place:

▶ Decision pending

▶ Continuation

▶ Stall.

Decision pending

Decision pending is a waiting period in which the decision has not been made. The reason could be that a key decision maker either was not present when the proposal was made or has not yet made up his or her mind; or that other, more pressing issues have arisen.

Continuation

Continuation means that the customer seems to be interested in continuing the relationship with you but makes no specific commitment regarding your proposal.

Stall

Stall is a situation in which the customer puts you off or seems evasive. A stall usually indicates a hidden objection. Stalls typically occur after you have asked for a commitment. Use the following tactics to handle a stall:

▶ Try to find out the real reason for the stall by using your questioning skills

▶ If the customer does not buy, find out why

▶ Get the objections out in the open and handle them, to determine the real reasons for not buying.

Concluding the call

Concluding the discussion usually takes 10 per cent or less of the total time of the conversation. But concluding effectively is critical to the success of the buying process because it enables you to gain the customer's commitment to future action. The steps for concluding are:

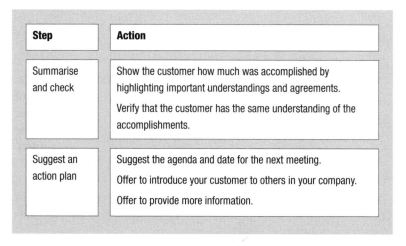

Step	Action
Summarise and check	Show the customer how much was accomplished by highlighting important understandings and agreements. Verify that the customer has the same understanding of the accomplishments.
Suggest an action plan	Suggest the agenda and date for the next meeting. Offer to introduce your customer to others in your company. Offer to provide more information.

Figure 28: Concluding the call

Benefits

Following this process for concluding:

► Allows you to see if you are on target

► Shows that you have listened to the customer

► Ends the discussion with an action step

► Keeps the dialogue open between you and the customer.

chapter eight **Connecting with customers in the digital age**

Interactive media marketing

If you think, or are led to believe that the Internet, WAP technology or interactive television is about to make traditional advertising and marketing redundant you are likely to be disappointed. Despite new technology, television, magazines and posters are still perfect for the passive, one-to-many, one-way awareness messages of mass marketing. However, they are making, and will increasing make, a major impact in the area of 'interactive marketing'.

Interactive media is fast becoming the new tool of customer-focused direct marketing. Consider what interactive really means – two-way. It is advertising you respond to – just like direct mail, coupon print ads, even direct response television commercials on a many-to-many format. It is likely that new interactive media will eventually revolutionise direct marketing, more than mass marketing.

Instantaneous and effortless response

Imagine how many more products would be ordered if all people had to do was click a mouse or a remote control, instead of mailing a coupon or picking up the phone! The powers of television with the targeting of direct mail or e-mail. Television works because of the lure of combining moving pictures with sound. Direct mail works because the only customers targeted are those who need your product. Imagine the power of both attributes together! During a commercial break, potentially every household could see a unique combination of adverts. These would have been selected on their known or calculated preferences. Viewers could then interact on a real-time basis.

Electronic mail instead of paper mail

The cost of paper, printing and postage for the typical direct mail package is increasing in cost. What's more, the cost of processing a response can easily be more expensive than producing the mailing. That means direct mail is only cost-effective for relatively high-value purchases. Therefore, imagine how many more applications there would be for electronic direct mail costing – just a few pennies per piece! However, before catalogues and direct mailers start disappearing from mailboxes, a lot has to change.

Interactive media consists of several competing technologies – all are imperfect

The World Wide Web is still painfully slow for most users, it is sometimes unreliable and has not yet been proven safe for credit card transactions in the mind of many customers. It is likely that direct response marketing will take hold in more reliable and secure proprietary networks such as AOL or other major ISPs. However, it is precisely because these networks are proprietary – open only to those with the necessary software and subscription ID – that they are criticised as interim technologies, at best.

Ultimately, the market will tell us which technology wins out. Perhaps even more important than perfecting the medium, however, is winning over the customer. Customers, even in the digital age, tend to walk to new technology, rather than run. Customers need a reward for doing something in a new way. More convenience, for example, plus perhaps, a financial incentive.

Consider that in the next few years the Internet will merge with the television. This new medium is currently referred to as 'web-casting'. Inside five or fifty channels, there will literally be a thousand, or a hundred thousand. TV quality digital video and audio will be 'piped' from a web site or web cast source directly into our homes on a real basis in the same way that e-mails, files and pictures are done now.

How are companies striving to win customers over to this new medium?

These examples are simple and constantly moving forward, but are useful in encouraging you to think about how your business might take advantage of interactive marketing.

Virtually every car manufacturer has a web site with lots of graphics and specifications of their models. In order to buy their product, you have to go back in time to old-style channels called 'dealers'. Imagine if these same sites could tell you – at the very least – which local dealers had which specific models in stock. And what if you could actually negotiate prices with dealers online, saving yourself the bad-taste-in-your-mouth unpleasantness of doing it in person? Consider PCs, practically every hardware and software company has a web site designed to dazzle you with their latest technology. But if you have a question about the old technology you're using now, you have to use an even older technology – the telephone – to call 'tech support' (and, of course, suffer the obligatory 30-minute wait on hold).

Imagine if you could log on to an online help centre, punch in your own personal ID code, and access information specific to your system. The online help centre would know the configuration of your system, so it could tell you, for example, exactly which upgrades you needed in order to run Windows 2000.

Imagine if you could log on to a clothing manufacturer's web site, upload your picture, and then see yourself dressed in the designer's latest creations right on your screen. If you happened to have detailed measurements on hand, the site could also 'fit' you into the most appropriate-sized garment, which could then be shipped for you to try on.

Millions of us go to huge home-improvement and wholesale-club warehouses. These places are designed for 'cash-and-carry' efficiency. But imagine if they had a 'virtual' store online, for the times you're too busy to stop by and are willing to pay slightly more to make a mail-order purchase. You could navigate the aisles, stocked just like those in the real store. And you could click on any item to see a close-up picture, specifications and price, and then click again to order.

The bottom line

Ultimately, the commercial success of interactive marketing will depend upon developing applications that actually reward the business or customer, in terms of added convenience, cost savings, and even fun. It's a safe bet that direct marketers will get to those applications first.

There's a big difference between identifying a segment that we want to move towards direct communication and developing a segmentation scheme that allows for multiple and ongoing targeting. For example, with business marketers, the desire for segmentation too frequently starts with a single focus request that is driven by a tactical need. Examples that you will recognise are as follows (I have listed them in increasing order of difficulty to segment):

► All companies that reside in a given geography (sales blitz).

► Customers who have purchased a certain product (upsell).

► Firms who are in this Standard Industry Code (SIC) and are larger than 100 employees in size (lead generation).

► Customers who have not purchased in the last year, are in a certain SIC and have responded to a direct mailing in the last six months (reactivation).

These requests come from sales or marketing groups that are faced with a specific tactical need. The request then lands on someone's desk for action and, if lucky, can be fulfilled if the data resides in the database and can be sorted and outputted without a major programming effort. More often than not, the data doesn't exist, can't be accessed or is in multiple files.

The real problem is that no one has taken the time to develop a comprehensive segmentation scheme – a subsequent list of customer attributes required – and then gone about building the database so that it can be queried and outputted in multiple ways. Unless this is accomplished, database marketing for business marketers will be a tortured process leading to unsatisfactory results.

Identifying the right data

Step back from the hectic pace and think broadly of the key data that you will need to satisfy 95 per cent of these tactical requests. In addition, what future information might be required in extracting a unique slice of customers or prospects? The benefits include having the correct customer and prospect attributes. Not only will you be able to respond to those tactical requests, but also, with good data, the opportunities for modelling and relevant communications and programmes significantly increase.

Following is a plan of attack to consider. It is sequential, as the first categories are essential building blocks, followed by more complex and difficult to gather customer attributes.

Transactional data

No segmentation scheme can work unless you know who your customers are, how much they purchase of what and when. This is not as simplistic as it sounds. Consider all the accounting information your company records on sales. It is probably too much detail for a marketing database, so don't just download all this accounting data to your files. Translate and consolidate this information into usable and actionable information. This should apply to payment/credit information as well.

Knowing the exact dates of payments isn't useful. Knowing that a customer is very slow to pay might be useful. The obvious point here is to extract transactional accounting information, not just bring over the entire file to your marketing database.

Company demographics

For all customer or prospect records the following basic attributes will lay a solid foundation for numerous segmentations:

▶ **Category code**: A four-digit code is usually a sufficiently descriptive definition unless your market is concentrated in several Standard Industry Codes, then going to the six or eight digit level may be appropriate. Remember, the SIC is currently undergoing revision, so be flexible with this field.

▶ **Company size**: There are two choices – sales volume or employee size. It is probably best to use employee size, as it is more easily obtained and more accurate than company revenue. Record employee numbers by site so that they can be rolled up to the corporate level.

▶ **Site type and linkage**: There are some standard definitions here such as branch, division and corporate headquarters. It is important that you take time to develop a site definition that fits your business as this might include plant, research centre, etc. Secondly, link the sites to a corporate structure, as referenced above, so that a roll-up to the enterprise level can be carried out to look at the customer picture.

▶ **Financial year**: For those selling situations that involve the customer needing to budget for your product or service, the knowledge of the fiscal year becomes critical, as this will drive the buying process and therefore your selling cycle. Most companies are on a calendar/fiscal year, but about 20 per cent are on a different fiscal year basis. In the consumer market this might also be relevant – for example in acquiring expensive items.

Relational demographics

The product or service that your company markets is also linked to selected facts about the customer or prospect. For example, if you're selling PVC resin (polyvinyl chloride), it is critical to know what type of process the customer employs (e.g. extrusion, rotational moulding, vacuum forming, etc.). The equipment that is in this plant may also make a significant difference in the communication offers and campaigns directed at the company. Sales people know and use this type of information every day, and therefore can be of great help in identifying the best attributes and possibly in the collection of the data.

Here are a few categories to help your thinking:

► Size of the site, machines, etc.

► Type of equipment in use

► Processes employed

► Competitors currently selling to the company

► Key industry trade shows attended by the customer

► Age of facility, equipment, etc.

This is an area for creativity, as the use of relational demographics will probably be something your competitors aren't using, this is known as 'stealth marketing'. Stealth marketing is developing a programme for a select group of customers/prospects that is based on targeting criteria that is not obvious. Like bad boxers, marketers telegraph their punches many times and a good defence or counter punch can easily be executed. To further the analogy; stealth marketing is like a blind side punch coming from an unexpected direction and landing with great impact.

Behaviour

You should be more concerned with the actual behaviour of customers and prospects not their awareness or opinions. Therefore, on the database there should be data fields that capture not only the 'touches' pro-actively directed at targets, but the response (behaviour) as well. The three pro-active touches are mail, phone and sales calls. In addition, capture fields should be set aside for other types of customer or prospect response, such as trade show visits, advertising response or customer service calls.

These records should be tied to individuals within a site and linked to the enterprise. Analysis can then be done on several levels to determine interest and activity. Many times when a need exists, several people within the site will request information and it is wise to remember the old phrase 'where there's smoke there's usually fire'. Admittedly, this requires much planning, feedback loops (particularly with sales and distributors) and discipline to record what communication is sent and what response occurs. But, if done well and tied to the preceding building blocks, it will produce an incredibly powerful tool for slicing out just the right group of customers or prospects and then communicating a highly relevant message that will get close to one-to-one marketing.

Needs

As opposed to the preceding attributes, the attempt to attach 'needs' to individuals or companies is more of an art than a science. Following are the main need attributes that are normally discussed.

Firstly, individual needs are important, as we don't sell to companies but to individuals. Most professional sales training programmes have a module that helps the sales person understand the driving motivation behind individuals. If your sales group uses such a model, then attach a field next to each contact name, that reflects the appropriate definition of motivation. The sales group then fills this field in on their laptop. This will reinforce their training and also serve to link them into the database concept. The usage of this information is powerful in the hands of a copywriter who will be able to craft a message that speaks directly to these types of motivation.

Secondly, marketers have tried to cluster companies into need based groups (e.g. need for just-in-time delivery). While I agree in concept with this approach, the question quickly becomes: 'How do you actually tag companies with the right label?' My experience is that you cannot do this cost-effectively for two reasons:

1. The input is from people within the company and multiple people may provide different inputs to your sales or customer service group. If you haven't been paying much attention to your customers lately, you may find that despite your quality products and good value, they're busy moving on to someone else.

2. It is commonly found that 69 per cent of customers leave a company because no one paid any attention to them. In today's aggressive marketplace, when marketers look the other way, someone else will romance their customers. As with personal relationships, if marketers take their customers for granted, even with the best of products and services, their customers will find another company to give them the attention they desire.

No longer is the customer watchword 'price'. Today's customers are driven by convenience. Customers are struggling to make their lives easier. If a customer's current company isn't delivering convenience; they'll find another one that will.

What does this mean for marketing? Today's desirable companies must know how to pro-actively make customers' decisions easier. The current and future customer trusts the firms that have their customer records in order and are willing to provide feedback on purchases and product/services utilisation.

Today's successful customer relationship programmes must include:

▶   Keeping customers informed when they are about to need a product or service

▶   Helpful reminders and suggestions

▶   Friendly, non-confrontational customer service

▶   Prompt attention to customer problems

▶   Customer service representatives who follow-up when they say they will.

The future of successful marketing is through improved customer service, by paying more attention to important customers. Consider these two important facts:

1. It costs five times as much to acquire a new customer than it does to keep a current one.

2. Retaining two per cent of customers annually has the effect of reducing operating expenses by 10 per cent.

A few years ago these findings would have had little impact. Until recently, the only numbers that mattered to Wall Street and the executive suite were gross margin, return on equity, sales forecasts and share of market. Today, knowing the true worth of an individual customer is critical to company survival. Why? Customers have more choices than ever before. Products and services are, for the most part, at parity levels and downsizing and global competition are also important factors.

As competition becomes ever keener, so too does marketing, thanks to technology. Today's advanced computer systems and user-friendly software have elevated marketing to a new level where measuring the true worth of a customer is possible. Armed with new technology (which did not even exist five years ago) savvy marketers can calculate the value of their customers in their database, communicate a customer's value to employees, and the customer, and track customers' behaviour over time.

Finding the true worth of a customer

To establish a customer's value, you must first find out your share of the customer's lifetime purchases in your product/service category. Secondly, you must learn the value of the customer's loyalty over the life of their relationship with the company.

As forward-thinking companies begin to measure customer lifetime value, many are gaining the added value of learning how to manipulate sales history, with an eye to predicting the future. Smart marketers are viewing their market in terms of potential value segments, and are weighing the merits of marketing strategies (ROI) and their ability to leverage customer lifetime value.

The challenge is how to cope with all the necessary data and how to develop the ability to capture transaction information. Measuring every customer contact means capturing a tremendous amount of data.

Since not all businesses have the luxury of capturing so much data, other means of identification and monitoring must be found. This includes predictive behavioural data driven from household self-described or appended data and estimates based on geography or consumption patterns applied to those remaining records. It is wise to remember that estimates based upon such methods are only estimates and cannot be considered accurate.

A variety of new software applications make it easier for marketers to analyse huge amounts of data. These include:

► Data warehousing (storing of large amounts of data)

► Data marts (summarisation's of data operations, sales, HR, etc.).

For real-time data interpretation, a variety of easy-to-use tools distribute data in executive-friendly information packets to designated areas of a company. They include:

► Executive information systems

► Decision support systems

► Online analytical processing

► Front-end query tools.

Software also exists to enhance customer service management through the creation of a hybrid system using the distributed customer information. A contemporary customer service database can provide customer histories to anyone who has contact with the customer at the time the customer needs help. These systems are available at all ranges of company size.

Having quality information at the point of customer contact is the key to delivering the quality of customer service demanded by today's customers. Being in a position to evaluate a customer's history and potential is essential if you are to remain of value to the customer. A successful customer service system must include quick access to the customers' history.

Share of customer

The battle for customer loyalty is also a battle for a greater share of each customer's purchases; this is often called 'share of requirements' or 'share of customer'.

Today's customers who are in the market for durable goods (such as computers or automobiles) are no longer multiple brand purchasers. They are multiple-brand 'considerers'. This change means that brand loyalty must be logically measured by share of consideration.

A stunning new automotive industry finding revealed why this standard is more useful than the old 'satisfaction' or 'repurchase' rate. According to the J.D. Power and Associates study, while 90 per cent of car owners claim to be satisfied with their current car, barely one third say that they will buy the same make that they now own.

Another recent study using panel data from MRCA Information Services of Stamford, Connecticut, USA, showed that a cross section of packaged goods brands had, on average, only a 31 per cent share of customers among their own high profit buyers. Of the eleven representative brands, the high-profit customer bought their favourite brand only about three out of every ten times. This means they bought competitive brands seven out of ten times! These studies underline the critical importance of targeting customers on a one-to-one basis.

Every customer contact point – whether it be telephone, personal contact, mail, fax or e-mail – must be kept current and complete within the database marketing information system. The loyalty of each customer will be determined by the correctness of this information.

The combination of customer historical transaction, service and activity information will be the foundation for developing a new 'potential code' that will identify the potential of each customer inside the database. When this code is coupled with the lifetime value, a customer service representative will know instantly which customers deserve more attention because they contribute most significantly to the company's bottom line.

Hopefully, you are now enthused to rethink the attributes captured in the marketing database. It will require hard work and time to build an advanced segmentation scheme. Just imagine not only being able to quickly respond to those requests, but more significantly, being able to model and analyse the database to identify new segments for increased sales and profits.

However, it is important not to ignore the basic principles of making customers feel special. Too often customers are greeted with a collection of recorded voices, telling them which buttons to push to access yet another menu of too often inappropriate choices. People find themselves reduced to bits of data in some huge computer, infinitely interchangeable with everyone else. If your marketing programme reinforces that sense of being just one small part of a great undifferentiated mass, how much customer loyalty can you expect from them in return? The good news is that this trend offers a huge potential competitive advantage for the business that can demonstrate palpable concern for each of its customers as real people, with widely differing needs and preferences. And ironically, it is those same dehumanising computers that can turn selling to 'markets of one'– or something very close to it – into practical reality.

Using segmentation, today's sophisticated database strategies let you focus on customers who are potentially most valuable to you. Segmentation enables you to use ongoing, targeted communications to create a loyal base of long-time customers, whose value to you grows over the years. It is the clearest path to relationship marketing – and the next best thing to one-on-one communication.

What is segmentation?

Segmentation makes it possible to break out the companies in your market universe into any of a number of different combinations, according to whatever criteria you choose. Its aim is to let you work with each segment separately, talking to each in terms of their specific hot buttons.

More specifically, market segmentation is a means of dividing your customer universe into a number of distinct groups, or clusters, based not on your products, but on their needs. The process consists of a number of steps:

- Defining your customer universe for segmentation
- Identifying the needs and concerns that drive their purchasing
- Comparing their needs/likely profit potential to your strengths; identifying areas of overlay
- Developing actionable segments based on clusters of similar customer needs
- Validating your segmentation model and hypotheses
- Assigning customers/prospects to segments tagged with firmographic and other profilers
- 'Grading' customers within each segment to project their profit potential
- Defining your best, most loyal and profitable core of customers
- Targeting resources proportionately to segments with best long-term profit potential
- Developing a marketing plan for each targeted segment, via an effective media mix
- Establishing measurements to track profitability by segment, against such quantifiable goals as expense to revenue ratios, repurchase and retention rates, product penetration, dollar volume and referrals.

What will you have when you've finished?

Upon completion your marketing universe will be divided into various groups, each consisting of customers who share common, defined clusters of needs, preferences and buying behaviours. You will also know:

▶ The net current and potential profitability of each segment, after the expenses associated with acquiring and servicing these accounts

▶ How much opportunity for further profitable development each presents, and from whom

▶ Where/how further development of your products and services can have the greatest impact

▶ The percentage of your marketing resources which should be allotted to each

▶ The kinds of messages and offerings to which each will most likely respond

▶ The media which will be most effective in reaching them, within each segment's budget.

Developing a marketing database

Market segmentation is an amazingly powerful means of organising everything you know, or can find out, about your most potentially profitable customers. That knowledge organised and preserved in a database will serve as a springboard for relationship management. This, in turn, is the surest way to build a growing customer base characterised by loyalty and profitability.

Ask the key question:

Why have these customers – whether consumers or companies – chosen your solution above all others?

Which of their needs have you particularly qualified and been willing to meet?

Start with your own employees. Ask those who know your customers best, such as account managers, sales reps and dealers, questions like:

- How does this customer's business, and particularly its purchasing cycle, work?
- Is it centralised or decentralised?
- How long is the buying cycle, from initial identification of needs to a purchase decision?
- Who (by job title) influences that decision, with what degree of clout, at what points in the cycle?
- What information do they need to do that, and when?
- Where might you improve your product offerings to help them with unmet needs?

This is information unique to your company. When you use it, your competitors' segmentation is unlikely to look anything like yours.

Next, find out what's available in industry research – for instance, from trade journals, government sources or professional organisations in your customers' fields. For additional 'data overlay' information, or to validate the data you have, such firms as Dun & Bradstreet are a resource. In some industries there are also very good syndicated reports available.

However, your best sources of data are the customers themselves. You can initiate ongoing, two-way dialogue directly with current customers, via such techniques as:

- Offering an inbound freephone number or help line
- Establishing user groups
- Publishing a market, or segment-specific customer newsletter, and interviewing customers for articles
- Scheduling advertising or direct mail with a response mechanism
- Querying visitors to your trade show booth
- Conducting surveys or focus groups.

You also need a reliable means for getting all of this information into your database. Remember that a well-designed, well-implemented database is a powerhouse of corporate memory. Every customer contact person in your company, from your service people to your telemarketers, should understand that part of their job is closing the loop, making sure that each pertinent insight is logged into the corporate database, through whatever process you devise.

Mining the database: Transforming data into information

However, capturing the information 'regionally' and storing it centrally is just the start. There is a big difference between raw data and usable information. The former is specific to individual companies, like the thousands of pieces of a jigsaw puzzle before it's assembled. To put it all together you need to identify patterns, specific needs and buying behaviours among customers and prospects and determine which of those patterns are common to significant groups.

If you're typical, 80 per cent of your customers buy from you for one or more of just a handful of reasons – usually, about four to six. What are those reasons? And how well do they coincide with the service values you have consciously worked on developing? You're also searching for other current or potential customers who 'look' as much as possible like those whose needs best coincide with your strengths, because it's within their ranks you're most likely to develop still more loyal, profitable customers. When you overlay the service values you've deliberately cultivated over the matrix of your customers' needs, you begin to see where your marketing emphasis should be.

You may want to segment your full universe of customers and prospects, or to limit the search to those involved with one product line, or even a single product. The process is infinitely flexible. In any case, there are two key questions:

1. What kinds of loyal customers are most interested in those service values that best differentiate you from your competitors?

2. What differentiates them from the mass of customers?

Art *v* Science: Making hard decisions with soft facts

Making each segment as unlike any other as possible is critical to effective segmentation. Here is another point at which the computer provides an invaluable aid. A well-constructed database, with analysis programs to slice and dice customer characteristics many different ways, gives you sophisticated tools for experimenting with a number of 'what if' scenarios to turn data into information.

Start with a list of needs and buying behaviours. Then query your database (supported as necessary through primary research) to find out how many customers cluster into groups that care about each of various combinations of those needs. Where you find larger numbers, you have identified 'need clusters' that are common to particular segments of your marketing universe and that's the raw material for needs-based segmentation.

Secondly, ask what easily identifiable characteristics the customers in each cluster have in common, in addition to those needs. You may, for instance, discover that many of them share geographical location, SIC, company size, or some other combination of characteristics.

In short, segmentation lets you define very specific needs-based market segments, into which you can divide your entire customer universe into present and potential needs.

Once you have computer output that shows you distinct portfolios of customers, each grouped around a different cluster of needs; you're ready for a 'reality' check. The process now becomes considerably more of an art (of interpretation) than a science.

There is no single 'right' segmentation scheme. Depending on the programs you choose to run, you might come up with any of perhaps a dozen alternatives. You now have to ask, 'Do these segments make sense, within the context of your company and your industry?' 'Do they gibe in important ways with what your sales people have encountered in the field, yet also provide new insights into customer thinking?' If so, you may have found your ideal segmentation.

In a sense you're called upon to function as a detective throughout the process. Beware of making unverified assumptions, based on what 'everybody knows' about customer needs. That's a starting point, but without careful customer research, it isn't possible to know for sure what those segments should consist of, or to identify the customer characteristics that surround each. You may make a number of interesting discoveries including some that fly in the teeth of conventional wisdom.

EXAMPLE

Imagine a segmentation plan for a medium-sized specialist tools manufacturer. One large 'segment' appeared, at the outset, to consist of small businesses whose stated primary need was for high quality in their supplies. Yet vast differences were identified in buying behaviour amongst these supposedly homogenous firms (Group A and B).

Some showed no indication of channel loyalty, switching suppliers every time someone announced a price promotion. Others had long-standing dealer relationships, some going back as long as 30 years, and their loyalty was to the dealer, not the product.

Further probing revealed that members of Group A were highly price-conscious, and valued the speed and ease of electronic purchasing. Vendor relationships, perceived as disruptions to their day, were seen as negatives. Group B, on the other hand, placed high value on human interaction and advice; as long as pricing was perceived as fair, it didn't have to be the 'best'. Clearly, attempting to market to these superficially 'identical' groups with a single plan would be self-defeating. They are separate segments, with very different needs, and should be approached as such.

Grading: Defining the economic value of each segment

The terms 'grading' and 'segmentation' are not interchangeable, although people too often use them that way. The two are entirely different processes and the distinction is important. Together, they create a very powerful economic model for customer selection, in order to achieve an optimal mix.

Unlike segmentation, grading is a strictly economic concept, carried out only within a segment, and/or for your entire customer base, to define various levels of economic value. It temporarily sets aside the issue of customer needs or other characteristics, and can usually be accomplished using historic account data and projected sales forecasts, most of which you already have in-house.

Grading is a means of estimating the revenue currently and potentially available from a given segment, allowing you to identify which groups are not only most responsive, but can also help you increase profits.

This, in turn, allows you to make intelligent decisions about resource allocation, to acquire and nurture more like-kind business by targeting those segments to which you can deliver superior value in a profitable manner.

All customers within each segment are divided into five 'grades', based on the revenue received from them over a given period of time. The top 5 per cent are rated AA; the next 15 per cent A; the next 25 per cent B; the following 25 per cent C; and the bottom 30 per cent D.

Determining projected lifetime value not just raw sales volume lets you fine-tune your grading system even further. To calculate lifetime value from anticipated revenue, subtract what it costs you to acquire, supply, and service this customer. Next, calculate the anticipated length of time you'll retain his/her loyalty, to project how much profit it is likely to bring you over the expected duration of the relationship (expressed in terms of Net Present Value).

You may find substantial surprises in this analysis. A demanding high-volume customer that buys primarily on price may be less profitable to serve than a low-volume customer who ranks high in terms of the other criteria above. Understanding this low-volume customer's priorities may point you towards other customers with similar needs, but larger budgets.

Grading can be a significant productivity tool, even in isolation. Not only does it allow you to direct your investments more effectively; it also serves as a foundation for a better field sales strategy.

Translating information into action

Information must be actionable, if it is to be of value to you. That means it must include a customer profile (most often consisting of demographics and buying behaviour – 'psycho-graphics!') that enables you to assign all of your customers to one or another of your defined segments. Unless you're both ready and able to use the results of all this effort to alter your marketing strategy, your money is probably better spent elsewhere. Segmentation only pays off if you use it to fine-tune your marketing programme.

If you have computed the lifetime value for each segment, you can now make a very scientific assignment of resources to customer groups. You can be selective in this process, if you choose, focusing on just a few segments – or even one. In fact, that may be a good way to validate your ideas before you institute any large-scale changes in your marketing strategy. The important thing is that you use the information to adapt marketing into a more customer-focused and less product-centred approach.

Often you can finance new marketing initiatives by re-deploying the budgets previously spent in pursuit of unprofitable business, because you can now recognise it for what it is. Screening out can be as important as targeting.

You can then assign an appropriate percentage of your marketing budget to each segment which merits pursuit, echoing the percentage of profits that segment has the potential to generate. Consider members with lower grades within a well-defined, profitable segment as areas of opportunity. You know that companies with a given cluster of needs and buying behaviours can be profitably attracted to your offerings and way of doing business. All that remains is to focus on expanding penetration there, bringing 'C's and 'D's up to the 'A' or 'AA' level.

To do this put your marketing imagination to work. Because you now understand the priorities of each segment so well, you'll also know how to determine the most potent messages for each, and the media mix that can best deliver it. In addition, because the economics of each segment are clear, you can develop a plan that matches communications alternatives to allotted budget on a cost-per-contact basis.

As a result, most of your money will be invested where the profit potential for developing loyal customers is the greatest. Whilst this strategy appears to be self-evident, it too seldom happens in real life decision-making, since quantification of potential profitability by market segment is sadly lacking.

What can you expect as a result of these changes and initiatives?

Segmentation helps you to understand what your customers need, so that you can actively manage and deepen your relationships with them, hopefully fostering greater loyalty, and, as a result, greater profitability. It also helps you to educate your organisation about different segment needs. This means that a team effort can be implemented to enhance delivery of products and services. It is easier to design and implement targeted offers likely to generate greater response, and this in turn will allow you to allocate your limited marketing resources among your most potentially profitable segments in ways that acknowledge and address their individual needs.

Loyalty schemes

There are many approaches to structuring customer loyalty programmes. Some programmes become biased toward the traditional promotional currency structure because it has been made so popular and obvious by travel companies, retailers, credit card issuers and telecommunications companies. Whether a programme has a promotional currency structure designed to reward customers or a series of soft benefits that hope to excite customers, there are some important decisions to be made early in the planning process.

Will your loyalty programme be overt or will it be covert?

Announcing a programme to the public sets a clear expectation in the mind of your customers. Customers believe that the programme is available to everyone and will be available on an ongoing basis. It's difficult to announce a test programme, because changes you may decide to make after the test period may be unpopular with customers. An announced programme is difficult to measure, in a traditional direct marketing sense. Pure measurement of a traditional direct marketing programme involves holding out a random control group that is consistent in composition to your test group. If you announce a programme you'll compromise measurement and probably skew customer involvement toward those whom already like your brand and are less likely to defect in the first place.

A covert programme is communicated to a group of customers, through the mail, telephone or the Internet. You select the customers and you also establish a control group. In this situation, it is best to avoid creating a 'club-like' theme to the programme. Customers have been 'clubbed to death' to a large degree and it is possible and more desirable to create an atmosphere of exclusivity and special service without labelling your programme a club. The successful implementation of a covert approach relies heavily on the creative positioning and execution. Focus on your special relationship with the customer, deliver extra service and, if possible, some tangible benefits, but avoid creating the perception that you'll continue this in perpetuity. You'll manage expectations while recognising your customers.

A clandestine approach like this supports more through the establishment of a control group, assuming you have a mechanism to track behaviour of your customers. For instance, telecommunications companies, retailers with private label credit card and catalogue companies have mechanisms in place to track customer behaviour. If you do not have a mechanism to track customer behaviour, set up a sample tracking study, which measures changes in customer behaviour and attitude through phone surveys. It is not as good as pure behaviour tracking but it is better than nothing.

In most cases a covert approach is best during the test and evaluation period. Some industries require a leap of faith right into an announced programme that is integrated in all advertising and communication and essentially becomes an integral part of the brand. Once a programme is announced, you lose the ability to effectively measure it.

Will you provide soft benefits or hard benefits?

This is the big question when it comes to loyalty programmes. Few companies can afford to give away tangible and meaningful rewards or awards, so decide this quickly. Travel companies, telecommunication companies and credit card issuers offer hard benefits because they can and because it's becoming a cost of entry. Many other companies cannot afford it in the long run (although a hard benefits approach makes a good, limited time promotion).

Don't assume that you're going to dream up some free soft benefits that will make a difference to your customer either. Explore the possibilities early in the planning process and make sure that you can, in fact, afford to do anything. Sometimes, simple but relevant communications several times over the course of a year can make a measurable difference.

Will enrolment be automatic or voluntary?

This is a consideration for an announced programme. Some marketers are tempted to take all customers and send them a 'welcome' message and fold them into a programme. Many customers just aren't going to pay attention to your announcement and it's my experience that roughly two-thirds of customers that are technically enrolled in an automatic programme are clueless about its existence.

Customers that must 'select themselves or get elected' and voluntarily enrol in a programme are much more inclined to engage in the programme and participate, and are much more likely to modify their behaviour as a result.

There are various shades of grey in between the pure automatic enrolment and the pure voluntary enrolment. It is possible to invite customers to join through the mail and provide an easy 'opt in' mechanism. Another option is to announce an automatic enrolment and provide a simple 'opt out' mechanism.

The bottom line is this: voluntary enrolment programmes will grow slowly but members will be much more involved; automatic enrolment programmes will grow quickly with disappointing member involvement.

Will redemption be voluntary or automatic?

This is an important consideration for promotional currency programmes. If customers have the option to redeem their currency whenever convenient, you're less inclined to realise incremental spending at redemption time. Customers will often wait until the time is right; they'll redeem and displace what would have been a paid sale. Automatic redemption can be structured to drive incremental sales at the time of redemption.

This is essentially a balance of what's best for the customer and what's best for the brand. But it is important to consider a balance between the two, because if you develop a programme that's great for the customer but bad for you, you're going to regret it. If you develop a programme that's great for you but a virtual yawn for the customer, it will fail miserably.

Following is an example of how to make it work. Let's say you're a retailer with an average time between customer visits of 45 days. A customer reaches a redemption threshold and you mail a certificate, as good as cash, for £25. To ensure that, on average, you're encouraging incremental behaviour, put a 30-day expiration on the certificate. You'll reduce the time period between visits and drive incremental business over the long run.

Use these key questions as a checklist if you're contemplating a loyalty programme. You can establish a heated discussion within your own organisation, which is probably a healthy thing to do at this point, rather than after you have launched.

chapter nine **The ten keys to outstanding customer service**

Introduction

This chapter is designed as a simple and straightforward list of truisms and sound bites regarding high levels of customer satisfaction and what that means in an organisation. Remember, the two most effective methods of generating increased sales and customer retention are to:

1. Give a customer such a superior experience that they have no reason to go or even look elsewhere.

2. Give them an incentive to spend more, return, refer or buy more frequently.

It is hoped that these statements will be useful in inspiring others around you to share your vision and commitment to the principles and practices in this book.

How to make every customer a special customer

S peed

P ersonalise

E xceed expectations

C ompetence and courtesy

I nformation

A ttitude – 'Can do'

L ong-term relationship

---

1. Whatever it is you do – do it fast

The need for speed

- ▶ Speed is competitive advantage.
- ▶ Everything is time-based.
- ▶ Time is the scarcest commodity in the world.
- ▶ When a customer says 'time is not important' – ignore them.
- ▶ FAST = **F**ast **A**ction **S**ecures **T**rust.

Speedy follow-up and fast service

- ▶ Fast service adds value.
- ▶ Speedy follow-up shows you care.
- ▶ The more time-sensitive your product, the greater the potential competitive advantage.
- ▶ Speed costs nothing, but has to be built-in.

2. Positive communications

People would rather buy from a friendly and enthusiastic trainee than an indifferent expert.

Talk the customer's language

- ▶ Cut out jargon, and explain things well.
- ▶ Aim to be understood.
- ▶ Take responsibility for your communication – the purpose of your communication is the response you get.
- ▶ Make written communications short, specific and simple.
- ▶ If in doubt, simplify.
- ▶ Talk benefits, not just features.

Treat others as you would wish to be treated.

Use side by side language

▶ 'I see what you mean'

▶ 'Let's see what we can do about this' 'I would be as concerned as you are'

▶ 'I'm sure we'll be able to find a solution' 'Do you see any possibilities that I haven't considered?'

Always say what you can do, or will do, not what you can't do or won't do.

Positive phrases get positive results

▶ I can...

▶ You can...

▶ I will...

▶ Will you please...?

▶ Could I ask you to...?

▶ So that...

▶ Here's what it means to you...

▶ Which means that...

3. The personal touch

Personalised service

► People like to buy from people.

► You build a business one customer at a time; one purchase at a time.

► Use the customer's name in all written communication.

► Courtesy, manners and politeness are keys to building trust, respect and loyalty.

► Use names regularly in conversation.

► Accommodate the customers special requests wherever possible (impossible is a subjective statement!).

► The first sale you make is yourself.

► Rapport is a skill that can be learnt.

► Non-verbal communication is the most important and quickest route to reaching people.

► Get to know your customers – all of them.

► 100 per cent attention at all times.

► Make every customer feel like your most special customer (not your only customer!).

4. Keeping customers

Customers are for life.... not just for Christmas!

Lost customers...

► 1 per cent die.

► 3 per cent move away.

► 4 per cent just naturally float.

► 5 per cent change on friends' advice.

► 9 per cent can buy cheaper elsewhere.

► 10 per cent are chronic complainers.

► 68 per cent go elsewhere because the people they deal with are indifferent to their needs.

► Make the extra-ordinary – ordinary!

Every year most businesses lose between 10 per cent and 30 per cent of their customers – and they don't even know who these customers are.

5. Turn complaints into opportunities

Welcome complaints!

► Complaints are opportunities in work clothes.

► Problems are wake-up calls for creativity and commitment.

► People complaining are people to value – they want to stay customers and are simply telling you how to achieve it and keep their custom.

► Get rid of nice customers – ask them to be critical!

► Be pro-active, not re-active to customer service issues.

Painful statistics...

▶ Only 4 per cent of dissatisfied customers tell us, 96 per cent tell other people.

▶ Each unhappy customer tells an average or 10 or more people (13 per cent tell 20 or more).

▶ Resolving a problem quickly will turn 95 per cent of unhappy customers into return customers.

▶ 40 per cent of your perceived customer service is how well you solve problems.

It is vital that to achieve customer satisfaction quickly... if you get the opportunity to fix a problem... you do it quickly!

Customers complaints are great fun

Here's how to deal with any complaint and turn it around:

G et the facts

R esponsibility

E mpathy

A gree a solution

T hank the customer for complaining

F U N – Follow-Up Now!

6. Create 'moment's of truth'

Manage the customer's experience

▶ Pay attention to small details – they are the most important ones.

▶ Pay attention to the peripheral functions – reception areas, phones, staff manners, parking, customer areas, stock, presentation, letter-heads, invoices, packing etc.

▶ Everything counts – each time you meet or contact (or don't contact!) the customer, your status in the mind of that customer is either improving or diminishing.

Customers want two things:

1. To be made to feel good.

2. Solutions to problems.

Treat every customer as your most important customer

▶ When you are talking to a customer – they are your most impor-tant customer.

▶ You only have one customer – the one you are dealing with now.

▶ Think of the value of a ten-year customer.

▶ You might have hundreds of customers – but they might have only one supplier or a one-off purchase.

The customer always comes first

C = Clear messages

O = OK attitude

M = Make people feel special

E = Energy

S = Standards of performance

1st = First four minutes and last two minutes.

7. Exceed expectations

The extra mile is never crowded

► The world is full of mediocrity.

► Any idiot can make something a little cheaper, it takes vision and commitment to make or do something better.

► Don't do anything if you can't do it excellently.

► Set or establish clear expectations – and then exceed them.

► Explain terms, prices and conditions clearly, early and honestly.

Under promise, over deliver

► Build a 10 per cent cushion into all your promises, quotes and statements of performance, and ...

► Deliver faster, sooner, better, cheaper, 10 per cent more than you promised. Don't ever be tempted to relax or pocket the 10 per cent difference. There is an old farmers' saying: 'You can shear a sheep many times, but skin it only once.'

► Whatever the customer asks for...the answer is YES!

► Do something extra...as standard.

Building champions

► Someone **who** might be a potential customer is a **suspect**.

► A suspect who '**qualifies**' and expresses specific **interest** becomes a **prospect**.

► A **prospect** who transacts **once** becomes a minor **client**, or customer.

► A **client** who comes back for a second or third time becomes a real **client**.

► A **client** that leads to other contacts becomes a **champion**.

► Every **champion** can lead you to **at least** three other customers.

▶ Think of the value of customers as **lifetime** customers and a **golden chain** of other prospects, and treat **everybody** as a £100,000 customer!

▶ Your customers are your best sales people.

▶ You already deal with your best customers.

▶ Customer satisfaction is not the objective – customer ranting, raving and ecstatic delight is!

▶ How often do your customers go **wow**!

8. Systems are as important as smiles

▶ Make quality your number one priority

▶ Customer service and quality is part of everybody's job.

▶ Lead by example.

▶ Set quality and customer service objectives and goals.

▶ Review progress regularly.

▶ Make quality and excellent customer service the most important thing by measuring and rewarding them.

▶ Define specifics for quality and service.

Nobody is ever motivated to do an average job.

Team-work: quality circles and improvement groups

Cross-functional groups should:

▶ Focus on what you do really well

▶ Focus on what you could do better

▶ Meet regularly

▶ Implement ideas fast and unaltered

▶ Learn as they progress

▶ Reward customer-focused innovation.

Get a plan and work the plan

- ► Measure everything – you're customers do!

- ► Ask 'What can be simplified, automated, standardised and stream-lined?'

- ► Have a 'Plan B'; know what could go wrong and know exactly what to do if and when it does.

- ► Let front-line staff fix their own mistakes, and learn from them.

- ► Delegate accountability with activity.

- ► Brainstorm regularly.

A company's greatest asset isn't on the balance sheet. It's the number of satisfied customers it has.

Serve internal customers as well as external customers

- ► Everybody has a customer.

- ► Everybody is a customer.

- ► Build teamwork into your organisation.

9. Follow-up and follow through

Who cares wins...

- ► Follow-up... just for the sake of it.
- ► Surprise the customer – show you're interested.
- ► It's not sold until it's providing value.
- ► Sell products and services that don't come back, to customers who do.

Ask 'how well are we doing'?

- ► It directs attention to the quality of your service.
- ► It gives you directional feedback.
- ► It motivates you!
- ► It draws your customer's attention to just how good you really are.

You won't know how well you are doing unless you ask.

Stay close to your customers

- ► Listen, listen, listen... and learn.
- ► Ask your customer how you are doing – regularly.
- ► Know your strengths and weaknesses.
- ► Know why people are satisfied – and why some people aren't
- ► Know why your customers are your customers.

Ask customers for feedback

- ► Telephone surveys.
- ► Follow-up after a transaction to check how things went.
- ► Questionnaires and surveys.
- ► Market research.
- ► Look at your sales statistics.

10. Deliver!

Competence wins every time

▶ Training is not a cost; it's an investment.

▶ Define what competent behaviour really means.

▶ Establish customer-focused standards of performance.

Get it right first time

▶ Simplify procedures to reduce errors.

▶ Standardise systems to ensure consistency.

▶ Think through processes and methods to pre-empt all situations.

When you are in contact with the customer, you are in contact with the whole organisation.

Define your job in terms of adding value to customers

▶ Traditionally – this sets limits not goals.

▶ To have real effect define your job in terms of customer satisfaction and an opportunity to add value.

▶ Define it on the basis of the principle that people love to buy, but hate to be sold to.

▶ Don't sell things...sell benefits.

▶ To customers it sometimes seems that people are friendly, polite, enthusiastic, creative, positive, intelligent and committed – except for the eight hours a day they spend at work!

▶ Empower people to create excellence for the customer through personal example, training, standards and respect.

When you define your job in terms of adding customer satisfaction and perceived value you will do it quite differently.

Give customers what they want...

Customers want to deal with people who...

- Are easy to do business with
- Treat them as individuals
- Know their business
- Are willing to do something extra
- Inspire confidence.

What your organisation must understand

- High levels of customer satisfaction equals survival.
- Outstanding customer service is not a 'nice-to-have' it is a 'must-have'.
- Customers expect high quality service, and can go elsewhere if they don't get it.
- It is too expensive to replace customers, even if it were possible.
- Managing and creating 'moments of truth' is the key.

Three final thoughts...

Outstanding customer service means creating good feelings and solving problems in ways that exceed expectations.

People make the difference; if the customer hasn't got a smile – give them one of yours!

It's not what you do... it's the way that you do it!

chapter ten **Worksheets, exercises and action plans**

Introduction

Any attempt to improve your relationship with your customers will require internal changes, actions and decisions.

This chapter comprises a collection of discussion exercises, check-lists and questionnaires that can be used during sales and management meetings to review and analyse your customer standards, satisfaction levels and relationship management. They are not intended to be used in any order or sequence, and all should be fairly straightforward to use. Please adapt them as required for your business or meeting objectives.

The individual worksheets may be photocopied for individual use, but not for distribution.

Customer service examples

Overview

Participants should work in small groups or syndicates and complete the questions as directed on the worksheet. Issues can then be discussed in a larger group.

This type of activity encourages people to begin to consider their experience or views on each aspect of customer service in a broad sense.

Procedure

1. Form participants into small groups of 3-6 people.

2. Distribute worksheet.

3. Ask participants to work as directed through the worksheet. Encourage participants to relate their stories as fully as possible – what happened – who said/did what etc.

4. Allow 15-20 minutes for groups to discuss and make a note of their experiences.

Examples of good and bad service – Worksheet

1. Working in a group discuss examples of good and bad customer service from information obtained **when you were a customer**, list at least three of each.

2. Be sure to examine each case in detail, identifying what impressed or depressed people in each case.

3. Transfer to a flip chart and select one of your group to present back.

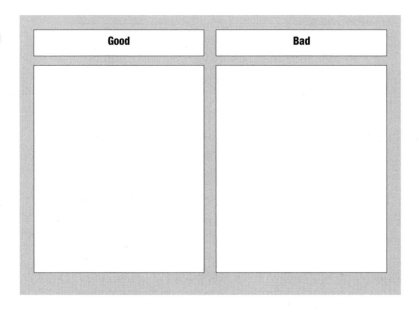

Good	Bad

Discussion points

▶ How many of the good examples are mistakes or problems by suppliers that are solved well?

▶ What are causes of dissatisfaction – small things or bad attitudes more than major problems?

▶ How many of the bad examples involve the attitude of staff serving?

▶ What are the similarities between the examples?

Defining excellent customer service

Overview

Participants use a simple but effective model to define customer relationship and service standards in their enterprise. This is a good and highly practical way of focusing on the different levels of service provided and identifying key elements or actions that produce delighted, satisfied and dissatisfied customers.

Procedure

1. Introduce the exercise by presenting and discussing the definitions of delighted, satisfied and dissatisfied customers as stated on the worksheet, perhaps using some examples drawn from your own experience.

2. Form participants into syndicates of 3-7 people.

3. Explain that each group should identify some elements or actions for each of the three customer experiences, with real life examples where possible, based on your own organisation, products or services.

4. Ask participants to work on flip chart pages for easy review.

5. Allow 10-15 minutes or longer for syndicates to generate as many ideas as possible.

6. Re-convene the main group in a circle around the flip chart.

7. Post up one page at a time and review key points.

Variations and notes

▶ Focus on generic examples.

▶ Focus on one aspect of service, e.g. handling complaints, telephone skills, etc.

Defining excellent customer service – Worksheet

Definitions

▶ Delighted customers are those whose experience exceeds their conscious or unconscious expectation.

▶ Satisfied customers are those whose experience equals their expectation.

▶ Dissatisfied customers are those whose experience in less than their expectation.

Task

Working in a group identify some elements or actions for each of the three customer experiences, with real life examples where possible, based on your own organisation, products or services. Transfer notes to flip chart paper.

Delight	Satisfaction	Dissatisfaction

Barriers to service excellence

Overview

Participants should work in small groups or syndicates and produce a list of common barriers to delivering high quality customer experiences and thus retention. Issues should then be reviewed and ideas for improvement discussed.

Procedure

1. Form participants into small groups of 3-6 people.

2. Distribute worksheets 'Barriers to service excellence 1 and 2'.

3. Ask participants to discuss and agree a score for each of the twelve elements. Ask them to note down examples on the second sheet.

4. Allow 15-20 minutes for groups to discuss and note their thoughts.

Barriers to service excellence – 1

The following statements (opposite) describe many organisations. Rank how true each statement is of your organisation and rate on a scale of:

1= Very true, 2= Somewhat true, 3= Not applicable, 4= Somewhat untrue, 5 =Totally untrue

Summary

12-21	Your organisation does not seem to be concerned with customers.
22-31	Your organisation seems to regard customers as an afterthought.
32-41	Your organisation seems about average in thinking about customers.
42-51	Your organisation seems concerned with customers but could improve its system for dealing with them.
52-60	Your organisation seems very customer-friendly.

	Score 1-5	
1	1-2-3-4-5	Policies established for the organisation's convenience
2	1-2-3-4-5	Over specialisation
3	1-2-3-4-5	No co-ordination of the service process
4	1-2-3-4-5	Remote policy and decision-making
5	1-2-3-4-5	Arbitrary service policies
6	1-2-3-4-5	More interest in cutting costs than in customers loyalty
7	1-2-3-4-5	Indifferent, unmotivated contact personnel
8	1-2-3-4-5	Scant creative problem-solving ability
9	1-2-3-4-5	Managers don't really know what customers want
10	1-2-3-4-5	Focusing on fixing, not preventing problems
11	1-2-3-4-5	Front-line contact people are powerless to solve most customer problems
12	1-2-3-4-5	Company dishonesty – promising more than can or will be delivered
Total		

Barriers to service excellence – 2

Barrier	How this might prevent service excellence in your organisation
Company policies that exist for company convenience and control	
Job specialisation	
No co-ordination of the service process	
Decision-making power that is too remote from customers	
Arbitrary service policies	
Top priority on cost containment	
Indifferent, unmotivated, powerless employees	
Not enough creative problem solving	
Failure to listen to customers	
'Customer service' is only a new name for the 'complaint department'	
Front-line contact people are powerless to solve most customer' problems	
Company dishonesty	

Gap analysis

To determine the difference between what you do and what your customers expect, complete the following analysis and fill in your answers on the table that follows:

1. Fill in your four most important outputs (products or service) in the space shown (A-D).

2. Visit or talk with at least three customers to determine what they expect for each of your listed product or service outputs, how important each expectation is, and how the customers rate your company in providing it.

3. Fill in what you learn about your customers and their expectations for each product or service listed.

4. Note how important each expectation is to the customer on the following scale:

   1= Unimportant/unnecessary

   2= Somewhat important

   3= Very important

5. Show how your customers rate your product or service in this area on the following scale:

   1= Does not meet expectations

   2= Meets expectations adequately

   3= Superior (exceeds expectations)

6. List any problems you uncover of which you were unaware.

Product/service

A: Product/service: _____

Expectation	Importance	Rating

B: Product/service: _____

Expectation	Importance	Rating

C: Product/service: _____

Expectation	Importance	Rating

D: Product/service: _____

Expectation	Importance	Rating

How you resolve customer problems

Describe two situations in which you dealt successfully with a customer problem. Then describe two situations in which your handling of a problem was unsuccessful.

Successful resolutions 1	Successful resolutions 2
What you said or did:	What you said or did:
Outcome:	Outcome:
What you could have said or done better:	What you could have said or done better:

Unsuccessful resolutions 1	Unsuccessful resolutions 2
What you said or did:	What you said or did:
Outcome:	Outcome:
What you could have said or done better:	What you could have said or done better:

Complaints as opportunities

A. Think of a recent negative service experience you've had as a customer. Describe it briefly below.

_____

_____

_____

_____

_____

_____

B. List three possible customer service opportunities (to keep the customer) in that interaction.

1. _____

2. _____

3. _____

Barriers to change

To identify barriers to change, tick the problems below that you are most likely to have, and then in Part B match each with the solution

Part A: Why people resist change

1 **Loss of control:** When people feel on top of things, change threatens them with losing control of their personal bailiwick or area of control/influence.

2 **Uncertainty:** Predictability is comforting to many people. Change brings uncertainty, which some people find threatening.

3 **Surprise:** We like new things but hate surprises. Sudden change is very unsettling to most of us.

4 **Habits:** We love our habits. They are efficient and don't require thought. Establishing new behaviour patterns is difficult.

5 **Familiarity:** The more we know things, the better we like them. (That's why companies spend a lot on advertising.) The unfamiliar is disturbing.

6 **Work:** New things usually mean more work (at least at the beginning).

7 **Competence:** People know that they can do what they already do. Change means they will have to master new skills, and they don't know if they will be able to do it.

8 **Ripples:** People fear that change in one thing will lead to change in others. (And they're right: that's the dynamic system.)

9 **Adjustment:** People are afraid it will take them a long time to adjust to any change.

Overcoming resistance to change

Part B

Place the numbers that you checked in Part A next to the strategies that will best fit them.

- Participation leads to ownership and commitment. Involve as many people as you can in the process.

- Communicate clearly, and often, the purpose of the change.

- Communicate exactly what you expect of people. Avoid surprises.

- Divide major change into manageable steps.
  (Make sure the first steps succeed.)

- Don't try to force people to pledge allegiance at the beginning. Let commitment grow.

- Be a model. Demonstrate your commitment to the change, and show your willingness to change yourself.

- Reward progress. Reinforce efforts to do things the new way.

- Find role models. Look for people who have already changed. Publicly commend them and let them guide others.

- Commit resources. Change takes time, energy and support.
  Make them available.

Increasing your customer awareness

The market-driven profile

Which of the following attitudes and practices describe you? If you answer 'no' to any of these practices think of things that you can change to become less product-oriented and more market-driven.

		YES	NO
1.	Do you have an organised method for regularly collecting and communicating to your customers and prospects?		
2.	Do you have an organised way of regularly talking with customers to uncover new needs or problems?		
3.	When you uncover problems with your product or services, do you feedback that information to the right people in your company?		
4.	Do you engage in joint planning and implementation programmes with your customers?		
5.	Do you participate in industry and community activities?		
6.	Are you committed to giving your customers what they want – even if it means stretching your company's normal operating?		
7.	Do you 'go bat' for your customers? That is, do you sell 'internally' to get upper management to bend or throw out the rules to accommodate special requests?		
8.	Are you obsessed with professionalism? Do you put a lot of effort into making sure that things are done right the first time? Do you convey this perfectionism to your customers?		

		YES	NO
9.	Do you keep abreast of industry/political/economic trends and think of ways in which they may impact on your customers?	☐	☐
10.	Are you an advocate of change or do you cling to the status quo?	☐	☐
11.	In the final analysis, do you see yourself as working for your company, as opposed to working for your customers?	☐	☐

Estimating lifetime value

Every business should establish a formula to rank customers based on a workable approximation of customer lifetime value. (This is determined by estimating the stream of future profits over some period of time, net of costs, and discounted at an appropriate rate, back to its Net Present Value.) Considering the challenges associated with determining lifetime value, most organisations will need to choose a list of 'proxy variables'. Such variables include (see opposite):

Proxy variables	Used as a proxy variable	Consider using for lifetime variable later
Past and expected future customer revenue		
Past and expected future customer profit (revenue minus cost of sales and servicing)		
Expectations about future loyalty		
Opportunities for up-selling and cross-selling		
Collaborative value – willingness to communicate/engage/participate/ respond to surveys, etc.		
Accounts payable – the speed at which the customer pays		
Time and effort customer devotes to the relationship		

Once you have chosen the variables that will help you estimate value, divide your customer base up into its constituent elements (e.g. business customers versus consumers, dealers versus distributors, etc.), and for each separate customer base:

► Rank order into five equal-sized groups, or quintiles

► Determine the percentage of profit to your firm represented by each quintile

► Explore ways to build a 'fence' around your top tier, that will help you focus on these customers and strengthen their loyalty

Complaint resolution

One of the most important, yet unrealised, opportunities in the strengthening of customer loyalty lies in complaint resolution. Such interactions are critical to how the customer will think of your organisation and discuss it with others. It is also an opportunity to determine the needs that your organisation might effectively meet, for this particular customer. Here are some key questions to answer:

Answer 'yes' or 'no' to the following questions. Repeat this activity one year after the initial date you complete it.

Date completed: Date in one year:	Now		One year from now	
	YES	NO	YES	NO
Does your company treat a complaint as an opportunity to develop a stronger relationship with the complaining customer?				
Do you use a customer's complaint as an opportunity to learn more about your customer and his or her particular needs?				
Is the experience and understanding – the customer knowledge – acquired in the process of handling a complaint effectively captured in the customer's record and made easily accessible to others who will work with the customer in the future?				
Does your company treat the resolution of a complaint as an opportunity to cross-sell or up-sell products?				
Are your most valuable customers recognised when they complain, and are they treated with appropriate additional care during the complaint-resolution process?				

Call centre checklist

Questions to measure your call centre effectiveness

To consider the issues regarding call centres, work through as many of these questions as possible. After answering them, begin the evaluation process. Where it's called for, consider using the columns on the right side of the page to show:

▶ Acceptable performance: Use a tick to show acceptable performance in this area.

▶ Need for improvement: 1, 2, or 3 to show urgency of need for improvement (1 being the most urgent).

▶ Ease of improvement: Use a '+' to show that the situation can be improved with existing equipment or software; use a '0' to show the need for further investigation and a '–' to show significant roadblocks ahead.

Work on improvements can begin with questions answered with a '1+'. Use the scoring system to prioritise next steps beyond those immediately actionable improvements (see over).

Acceptable performance ✔

Need for improvement 1-3

Ease of improvement + 0 –

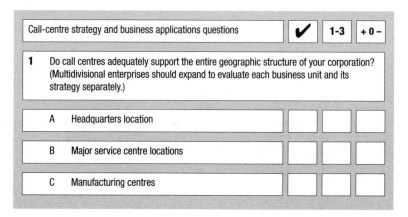

Call-centre strategy and business applications questions	✔	1-3	+ 0 –
1 Do call centres adequately support the entire geographic structure of your corporation? (Multidivisional enterprises should expand to evaluate each business unit and its strategy separately.)			
A Headquarters location			
B Major service centre locations			
C Manufacturing centres			

	✔	1-3	+ 0 −
D Processing centres			
E Claims centres			
F Retail locations			
G Sales offices			
H Independent distributors			

2 What are the lines of business in the corporation and your strategies for them?			
A Within the lines of business, what are the functions and services provided?			
B For the services provided, what are the origins of the customers?			
C What are the identification, segmentation, and entitlement approach for the customers of each line of business?			
D What is the business value and strategy for this line of business, e.g. growth, retention, entering new market, cost avoidance/reduction?			

3 What is the reporting structure of the lines of business and their service centres?			
A Centrally managed?			
B Geographically distributed management?			
C Are the potential synergies across these areas adequately used?			

		✔	1-3	+ 0 −

4 Describe growth needs and strategies, opportunities, and issues

A	Growth by application?			
B	Growth by geography?			
C	Growth by services offered?			
D	Major business initiatives by date and phasing?			
E	Adequacy of infrastructure to support initiatives?			

5 Describe hiring, training, staffing, work-force scheduling methods

A	What is the distribution of agent skills, and where do they reside?			
B	Does the firm balance its agents' skill use across the enterprise?			
C	Are labour rates, overtime, and time-zone shifts optimised?			
D	Is management of equipment and resources optimised?			

6 Are human resources approaches shared?

A	Common hiring?			
B	Common training?			
C	Common online and offline support materials?			

Operations and technology questions	✔	1-3	+ 0 –
7 What is the organisation of customer-information technology?			
A How are client record databases organised?			
B Where are they physically located?			
C How are the screen-based applications organised and offered to users?			
8 What is your communications infrastructure?			
A What is the architecture of the current voice network?			
B Common arriving traffic?			
C Common internodal tie line?			
D Virtual facilities?			
E Numbering plan across sites?			
F Adequacy of bandwidth for peak volumes?			
9 Review call management data: time-based performance statistics on all applications at the summery level by site			
10 Review 'from' and 'to' relationships for all cross-site transfers			
11 Review adequacy and currency of current disaster-recovery plan			
12 Review strategy for cross-site load balancing			
13 Overview time-of-day, day-of-week operational rules by site and application			
14 Map and evaluate voice-response infrastructure information			

15	Review usage data on VRU

16	Describe skills distribution of calls and agent assignments

17	Describe current management methods used for networking and ACDs, including management reports

18	Describe major seasonality of traffic by site and application

19	Assess computer telephony integration (CTI) applications, by flow and by application location

20	Identify top five areas of management dissatisfaction with current call centre operations

Provided courtesy of Lucent Technologies, formerly the systems and technology units of AT&T. Developed by Joe Righter, Lucent Director of Call Centre Advocacy.

The call centre 'reality check'

Perhaps the only real measure of any call centre is provided thousands of times each day by customers. Customers reward 'good' performance and punish 'bad' performance. Mystery shopping is one of the most powerful ways of understanding your 'real world' performance. It can provide a qualitative analysis that, when coupled with the centre's statistics, provides a far more 'real' view of the call centre through the customer's eyes. Don't talk or think about what should happen, or you think happens, measure what really happens.

Set a date for carrying out mystery shopper calls: _____

Here are some suggested steps to implementing a mystery shopping survey:

1. Planning the 'reality check'.

Description

▶ Choose a number of calls that will be achievable while providing a representative sample of the call-centre volume.

▶ Schedule the test calls over a variety of times that reflect call volumes (if half the calls are typically received between 8.00 and 11.00 am, make sure half the test calls are during that time period).

▶ Be sure to include peak times, key break times, late nights, and weekends (if more than one centre is employed, sample each proportionately).

▶ Create tests that represent different customer types and/or customers of different value or importance to the firm. Observe the different levels of treatment, if any.

▶ Recruit test callers who represent the caller population. Consider recruiting from outside the employee population, if necessary.

▶ Assure service reps that individual performance is not being monitored as part of the study. If necessary, sanitise the record to exclude service representatives identifying data.

2. Benchmarking against competition

Description

▶ On at least a semi-annual basis, conduct a scaled-down version of the assessment with each of your company's three to five most important competitors. Use objective questions that will provide directly comparable statistics to benchmark your call centre against the competition.

▶ Solicit information via mail, fax, or e-mail. Monitor your competitors' response times. Focus on the attitude, helpfulness, friendliness, and thoroughness of the competitors' responses. Consider using stopwatches to time total call duration and hold times.

3. Developing an analysis tool

Description

▶ No two call centres are alike. Develop a simple, single-sheet call assessment that can be used immediately on completion of each call. Keep the evaluation to no more than ten or twelve questions.

▶ Make the questions quantifiable when possible – answered either 'yes' or 'no' on a 1 to 5 point rating system so comparison can be drawn between time of day, specific call centre, customer type etc.

Checklist for measuring call quality

Listen to ten or more randomly chosen calls placed to your call centre. (Be sure to let both customers and operators know you may be listening in.) Evaluate those calls based on the following criteria:

Customer identification

▶ How well did the representative demonstrate knowledge of the caller or his situation?

▶ Did the system automatically identify the caller and link to their customer record?

▶ Was the welcome and problem definition brief, helpful, and to the point?

▶ Was the quality of the greeting friendly and informative?

▶ Were the prompts (options) clear and easy to understand?

Customer differentiation

▶ Was any unique or personalised welcome greeting employed once identification was complete?

▶ Did the agent reflect any knowledge of the caller's prior relationship with the company?

▶ Was the customer information used to speed the process (e.g. 'Shall I ship that to…?')?

▶ Were probing questions asked to gain further knowledge of the customer's behaviour towards, or their relationship with, the company?

Customer interaction

- ► Was the call answered promptly and appropriately?

- ► If a transfer was required, did it happen in a reasonable number of seconds?

- ► Was there any 'dead air', or extended hold periods?

- ► If so, was the 'hold time' used to provide appropriate information?

- ► Were 'opt-outs' provided prominently where appropriate (e.g. 'To reach a live operator...' or 'To leave a message instead...?')?

- ► Did the first person to speak with the customer solve the problem completely?

- ► Was the customer asked for any information that should have already been known?

- ► How long does it take to respond to specific requests by postal mail, e-mail, or fax?

Customisation

- ► Were agents empowered to vary from the scripts or rules at all? For valuable customers?

- ► Did customer information transfer along with the call, or did the conversation start all over again with the new agent?

Customer commitment survey

To evaluate your organisation's culture on the key factors in customer-driven service, rate the statements below on the following scale:

1 = Never, **2** = Rarely, **3** = Sometimes, **4** = Usually, **5** = Always

Then complete your profile index at the end of the evaluation.

Customer orientation	Circle your rating
1. Taking care of our customers is a top priority in our organisation – more important than costs.	1 2 3 4 5
2. We 'listen' carefully to our customers' needs through our informal feedback systems and act on this information.	1 2 3 4 5
3. We have a formal process in place to determine our customers' wants and expectations, now and for the future.	1 2 3 4 5
4. When we lose a customer we know why, or we find out why.	1 2 3 4 5
5. Our repeat business exceeds the industry average.	1 2 3 4 5
6. Our day-to-day activities are in harmony with our values and goals about customer satisfaction.	1 2 3 4 5
7. My managers' concerns and activities have convinced me that customer care is important.	1 2 3 4 5
8. Our customers are advocates in our organisation.	1 2 3 4 5

Manager's orientation	Circle your rating
1. Our managers 'walk what they talk'.	1 2 3 4 5
2. The predominant attitude around here is risk-taking, rather than defensive.	1 2 3 4 5
3. Managers give workers the responsibility and authority to take care of customers.	1 2 3 4 5
4. People think 'competition' means other companies, not the person down the hall.	1 2 3 4 5
5. We see ourselves as customers and suppliers in our work relationships with each other.	1 2 3 4 5

Co-operation/integration	Circle your rating
1. People at all levels can participate in decision making.	1 2 3 4 5
2. Supervisors and managers in different departments work well together.	1 2 3 4 5
3. Very few things fall through the cracks because the left hand doesn't know what the right hand is doing.	1 2 3 4 5
4. Our systems make clear who has responsibility for what tasks.	1 2 3 4 5
5. The organisation's goals are set at the top, based on our mission, and are clear and achievable.	1 2 3 4 5

6. Results and goals are set at the top, based on our mission, and are clear and achievable.	1 2 3 4 5
7. In every department we have clear measures and tracking systems to tell us how we are meeting our customers' requirements.	1 2 3 4 5

Attitude and skills	**Circle your rating**
1. What happens in the organisation really matters to all our people – executives and workers alike.	1 2 3 4 5
2. People feel responsible, needed, and empowered to do what needs to be done to take care of our customers and keep them satisfied.	1 2 3 4 5
3. Our customer service representatives know how to identify/solve service-related problems.	1 2 3 4 5
4. Problem-solving skills are used in every department and are standard operating procedure.	1 2 3 4 5
5. Our managers and supervisors have the skills to influence others, communicate effectively, and motivate and lead subordinates, particularly through periods of economic challenge and change.	1 2 3 4 5

Costs/prevention/results	Circle your rating
1. Our focus is on preventing problems rather than fixing them.	1 2 3 4 5
2. We regularly collect data on the costs of waste, rework, errors, and other elements of poor service quality.	1 2 3 4 5

Scoring and interpretation

Add up your scores, and interpret the total as below:

113-140 Your corporate culture seems very customer-oriented.

85-112 You seem personally committed to service excellence, but you need to get your system in line.

57-84 You may recognise the importance of customers, but your organisation doesn't seem to be acting this way.

28-56 You and you organisation seem to be interested in other things instead of service excellence.

Customer feedback analysis

Complete the following table to summarise the customer's importance versus actual performance or perception of service. The higher the value C, the better you are at creating satisfied customers. Plot the data on the grid to clearly highlight areas of strength and 'opportunity'.

(1=poor, 10=excellent)

Element of service/ performance or perception	A Importance to customer 1-10	B Performance rating 1-10	C Variance B-A
1.			
2.			
3.			
4.			
5.			
6.			
7.			
8.			
9.			

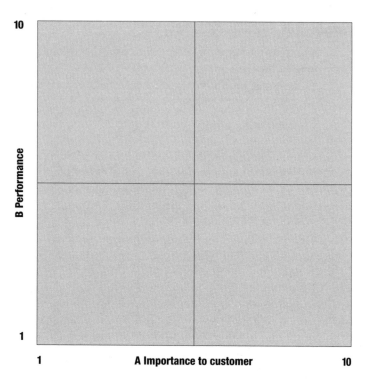

Integrating products

Instructions

1. Get together with a group of four or more people.

2. Brainstorm as many strategies as you can for differentiating one of the following products:

   - Paper clips
   - Computer disks
   - Insurance
   - Soft drinks
   - Children's clothes retailer
   - Dry cleaner
   - Garage (car/vehicle) servicing
   - Natural gas
   - Package delivery.

3. You may not change the product itself; instead, focus on the integrated product, such as delivery, customer relationship, billing, references, and value-added features.

4. When you have finished generating ideas, look over the list and try to find something useful, or something to improve on, in each.

The integrated product

Brainstorm ways to differentiate your product/service completing the three parts of this diagram.

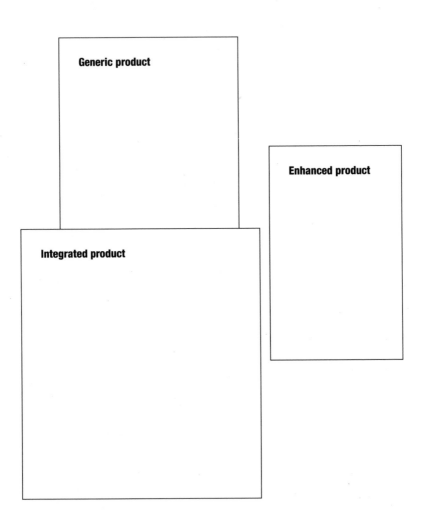

Generic product

Enhanced product

Integrated product

Customer service business plan

Answer the following questions:

1. What is our mission statement? A mission statement should be a summary of all the following points as well.

2. What product do we produce? What are the components of the integrated products-services, distribution, support, relationship, etc?

3. Who are our customers? What are the major sub groupings of customers, or market segments?

4. Where are our customers? Geographically? In terms of level in their organisation? How many steps are there between them and us? How do they get our products?

5. What do our customers buy? How close is it to what they need? How do we know?

6. What is our relationship with our customers? How do we know they are getting what they need? How do they learn how to use our products?

7. What do they do with what they buy?

8. Who are our known competitors? Who else provides products or services that could be substituted for ours in the customer's eyes? Who will our competitors be tomorrow?

9. What is it that our customers most value about our organisation (not just our products)? About our competitors?

10. What trends are there in our customers' businesses or lifestyles that are likely to change what they will need from us?

Common sources of service problems

Symptoms	Causes	Possible solutions
1. Human		
High turnover	Lack of standards	Revise job description
'It's not my job'	No accountability	Appraise people on customer satisfaction
Poor service	No rewards for good service	Reward people for good service
Numerous second requests	Priorities unclear	Make service standards clear
Lack of courtesy		
2. Developmental		
Improper responses	Improper training	Train employees in importance of customer and complaint handling
Inefficient investigations	No rewards	Cross training
Employees investigations	No career paths	Reward desired behaviour

Symptoms	Causes	Possible solutions
3. Structural		
Misdirected calls	Roles not clearly defined	Centralised contact point
Complaints not responded to	Conflicting missions	Ombudsman
Employees saying others aren't doing their jobs	People not given enough power	Co-ordinated goals
Nobody knows to whom problems should be referred		Decentralised authority
Surprises		Team building
4. Measurements		
Too much attention paid to irrelevant factors	Customer satisfaction not measured effectively	Ticking system for customer satisfaction and complaints
Nothing done to increase customer satisfaction		Measurement focused on behaviour
No accountability		
Customer satisfaction not measured		

Symptoms	Causes	Possible solutions
5. Support and communication support		
Inadequate capacity	Database not integrated	Upgrade support system so that the first contact can resolve 95 per cent of the problem immediately
Callers don't get through	Systems not user-friendly	
Too much downtime	Too much paperwork	
Large mail backlog	Poor follow-up systems	
Customers call twice for the same problem		
6. Analytical systems		
Too much time spent on fighting fires	No prevention system	Get contact data from each location
No data on why people patronise	No information on root causes	Track transactions

Symptoms	Causes	Possible solutions
7. Design and strategy		
Frequent customer complaints that services don't meet their needs	Lack of research	
	Lack of training	
	Contact people don't support company policies	
	Designs that please other departments instead of customers	
8. Implementation		
New crusades every quarter	Lack of strategy	Focus on how to satisfy customers
Conflicting goals	No planning	Limit numbers of new programmes
Progress has run out of steam		

Symptoms	Causes	Possible solutions
9. Internal communication		
Customers given wrong information	Not enough time to communicate	Survey employees
Contact people can't explain or politicise	No feedback	Employee newsletter
Contact people get news from customers	No timely written communication	Hold staff meeting on services
Employees look dumb to customers	Employees think management does not care	Employee ombudsman
10. External communication		
Unnecessary enquires	Failure to explain services to customers	Customer education

The cost of poor service

To estimate how much poor service costs your organisation, calculate the following:

Lost revenue	Your costs
1. What an average customer spends in a year	
2. The number of customers lost each year (for the average company, 25%)	
3. The revenue lost from lost customers (1x2)	
4. Lost revenue from people ex-customers talk to (3x10)	
Labour costs	
5. Time redoing things not done right in the first place	
6. Time spent on warranty repairs	
7. Time spent apologising to customers	
8. Time spent responding to government agencies, consumer complaint bureau etc.	
Other costs	
9. Cost of shipping express instead of regular	
10. Cost of collections from angry customers who refuse to pay	

Other costs *(continued)*	
12. Legal costs	
13. Telephone costs for apologising, explaining, etc.	
14. Postage costs for reshipping, apologising, explaining, etc.	
TOTAL (add numbers 3 through to 14)	

Customer dynamics

On a scale of one to ten, rate your company on the following measures of service quality.

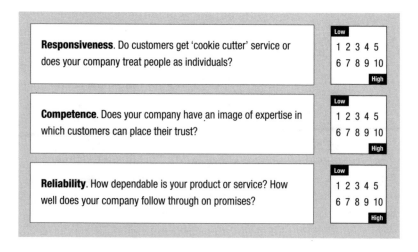

Responsiveness. Do customers get 'cookie cutter' service or does your company treat people as individuals?

Low
1 2 3 4 5
6 7 8 9 10
High

Competence. Does your company have an image of expertise in which customers can place their trust?

Low
1 2 3 4 5
6 7 8 9 10
High

Reliability. How dependable is your product or service? How well does your company follow through on promises?

Low
1 2 3 4 5
6 7 8 9 10
High

Relationship. How well does your company show customers that they care and want long-term relationships?

Low
1 2 3 4 5
6 7 8 9 10
High

Accuracy. How well does your company avoid mistakes, especially expensive or time-consuming mistakes?

Low
1 2 3 4 5
6 7 8 9 10
High

Personal service. How well do service representatives and other front-line people, show customers that they are special?

Low
1 2 3 4 5
6 7 8 9 10
High

Courtesy. Does everyone in your company treat customers with this – the most basic ingredient of human interaction and service?

Low
1 2 3 4 5
6 7 8 9 10
High

Active listening. Are people in your company good listeners, especially when it comes to customer problems?

Low
1 2 3 4 5
6 7 8 9 10
High

Perceived value. Does your company give customers good value and make them aware of that value before and after the sale?

Low
1 2 3 4 5
6 7 8 9 10
High

Professional appearance. Is your company aware of the importance of making a positive impression with a clean, safe, well-maintained place of business?

Low
1 2 3 4 5
6 7 8 9 10
High

Keeping in touch. Does your company make an effort to stay close to its customers and solicit their opinions?

Low
1 2 3 4 5
6 7 8 9 10
High

Management discussion points

1. **Customer share**

   ▶ What percentage of your customer's total expenditure do you receive?

   ▶ How might a customer spend on this area over the next five years?

   ▶ What percentage of your total sales volume do your top 10 per cent of customers contribute?

2. **Customer charm**

   ▶ How many customers have you lost in the past 6-12 months?

   Number of accounts_____

   Value   £_____

   Percentage of whole _____%

3. If you were prevented (by law) in attracting 'new' customers, so that all future sales had to be generated from existing customers or referral, what three things would you change first in your interaction with customers?

   1. _____

   2. _____

   3. _____

Sales development discussion points and questions

These questions are designed for testing and applying CRM principles to your sales and marketing development. They are designed to be used by sales managers, account managers and marketing executives. It is intended that they be best utilised in a business to business context, although they could be adapted for more retail/consumer orientated businesses.

1. Think strategically

▶ How far ahead do you set objectives for your business development pipeline and accounts, on average?

▶ For one or more named accounts, what is the estimated total annual spend on your area of business?

▶ What percentage of this do you currently win?

2. Planning and review

▶ Do you produce an annual or quarterly account plan?

▶ Describe how this is used and reviewed?

▶ Do you involve the customer in this planning phase?

▶ On average, how many hours per week do you spend planning, preparing and researching business development activity?

▶ What would you expect the benefits of better planning to be?

3. Set challenging account objectives

▶ For one or more named accounts, what is the annual sales gain from the last financial year to this year and projected from this financial year to the next?

▶ For one account only, complete the table for different product, service or solution areas.

Focus/account name	Total sales revenue last financial year	Projected sales revenue this financial year	Projected sales revenue next financial year

► How often do you set and review business development and personal goals?

4. Build a relationship matrix

► For one of your key accounts, summarise your key contacts as they exist now in the table below.

Name	Position	Average contact per three monthly period	Status of relationship: 0, +, ++, +++

► What gaps exist in your relationships?

5. Manage multiple buying influences

▶ For one of your key accounts, draw an account 'map'. This is a diagram showing all the major contacts and influences involved in your business area or decision making process (even those with whom you have had no contact) and how they interrelate and connect.

6. Create business needs and demonstrate tangible added value

▶ Unless you sell purely commodity items, most major purchasing decisions are not made solely on price. It has been found that business opportunities and objectives supposedly lost on 'price' may have in reality been lost because of one of the following reasons:

- Lack of demonstrable added value to justify a higher initial cost price
- Complacency by the business development person or account manager
- Poor account management
- Inadequate qualifying of the customer and business development process.

▶ Consider the last few business development opportunities that did not conclude positively. Which one of these elements is the most likely root cause?

▶ How can this be prevented in any future business development opportunities?

7. Anticipate and answer objections and obstacles

▶ Describe the typical steps that you would go through in closing a major business development opportunity. For example, how would you deliver or present your proposal? What would happen next?

▶ What are the most common objections, questions or concerns that customers raise during the later stages of the business development process or when reviewing your organisations performance?

Summary

Excelling and managing customer relationships is the future of your business, or any business. Product and service advantages can come and go, price and marketing promotions can be effective, but they are usually expensive and increasingly their results are less reliable and more short-term. Price-led marketing is also unlikely to be sustainable in the long term.

▶ The secret is to know who your customers are – all of them.

▶ Get to know what your customers want – individually and as associated groups.

▶ Work to make every customer feel special – at every opportunity.

Remember that there are three S's in successful customer relationship management:

▶ Standards

▶ Systems

▶ Skills

Work constantly to improve your standards. Implement systems that allow you to track and manage customers, and create a skill level and attitude in your staff that makes customers go WOW! After all, the purpose of a business is to create and keep a customer, everything else is detail.

Thorogood publishing

Thorogood publishes a wide range of books, reports, special briefings, psychometric tests and videos. Listed below is a selection of key titles.

Desktop Guides

The marketing strategy desktop guide	*Norton Paley* • £16.99
The sales manager's desktop guide	
	Mike Gale and Julian Clay • £16.99
The company director's desktop guide	*David Martin* • £16.99
The credit controller's desktop guide	*Roger Mason* • £16.99
The company secretary's desktop guide	*Roger Mason* • £16.99
The finance and accountancy desktop guide	*Ralph Tiffin* • £16.99
The commercial engineer's desktop guide	*Tim Boyce* • £16.99
The training manager's desktop guide	*Eddie Davies* • £16.99
The PR practitioner's desktop guide	*Caroline Black* • £16.99
Win new business – the desktop guide	*Susan Croft* • £16.99

Masters in Management

Mastering business planning and strategy	*Paul Elkin* • £19.99
Mastering financial management	*Stephen Brookson* • £19.99
Mastering leadership	*Michael Williams* • £19.99
Mastering marketing	*Ian Ruskin-Brown* • £22.00
Mastering negotiations	*Eric Evans* • £19.99
Mastering people management	*Mark Thomas* • £19.99
Mastering personal and interpersonal skills	
	Peter Haddon • £16.99
Mastering project management	*Cathy Lake* • £19.99

Business Action Pocketbooks

Edited by David Irwin

Building your business pocketbook	£10.99
Developing yourself and your staff pocketbook	£10.99
Finance and profitability pocketbook	£10.99
Managing and employing people pocketbook	£10.99
Sales and marketing pocketbook	£10.99
Managing projects and operations pocketbook	£9.99
Effective business communications pocketbook	£9.99
PR techniques that work	*Edited by Jim Dunn* • £9.99
Adair on leadership	*Edited by Neil Thomas* • £9.99

Other titles

The John Adair handbook of management and leadership
Edited by Neil Thomas • £29.95

The inside track to successful management
Dr Gerald Kushel • £16.95

The pension trustee's handbook (2nd edition) *Robin Ellison* • £25

Boost your company's profits *Barrie Pearson* • £12.99

Negotiate to succeed *Julie Lewthwaite* • £12.99

The management tool kit *Sultan Kermally* • £10.99

Working smarter *Graham Roberts-Phelps* • £15.99

Test your management skills *Michael Williams* • £12.99

The art of headless chicken management
Elly Brewer and Mark Edwards • £6.99

Exploiting IT in business *David Irwin* • £12.99

EMU challenge and change – the implications for business
John Atkin • £11.99

Everything you need for an NVQ in management
Julie Lewthwaite • *£19.99*

Time management and personal development
John Adair and Melanie Allen • *£9.99*

Sales management and organisation   *Peter Green* • *£9.99*

Telephone tactics   *Graham Roberts-Phelps* • *£9.99*

Business health check   *Carol O' Connor* • *£12.99*

Companies don't succeed people do!
Graham Roberts-Phelps • *£12.99*

Inspiring leadership   *John Adair* • £24.99

The book of Me   *Barrie Pearson and Neil Thomas* • £24.99

Thorogood also has an extensive range of reports and special briefings which are written specifically for professionals wanting expert information.

For a full listing of all Thorogood publications, or to order any title, please call Thorogood Customer Services on 020 7749 4748 or fax on 020 7729 6110. Alternatively view our website at **www.thorogood.ws**.

147730